Am I Doing This Right?

Am I Doing This Right?

Foundations for a Successful Career and a Fulfilling Life

Tony D. Thelen
Matthew C. Mitchell
Jeffrey A. Kappen

BUSINESS EXPERT PRESS
Leader in applied, concise business books

First published in 2022 by
Business Expert Press, LLC
222 East 46th Street, New York, NY 10017
www.businessexpertpress.com

ISBN-13: 978-1-63742-317-2 (paperback)
ISBN-13: 978-1-63742-318-9 (e-book)

Business Expert Press Business Career Development Collection

First edition: 2022

10 9 8 7 6 5 4 3 2 1

*This book is dedicated to everyone who has ever wondered
if they were doing things right.*

Description

This book was written for everyone who has ever wondered, *am I doing this right?* when thinking about their lives and careers. Leveraging the collective experience of hundreds of professionals, this book is the ultimate early-career desk reference! When readers finish reading this book, it is not the end, but the *beginning* of a successful career and a fulfilling life. Write in the margins, highlight key insights, answer questions, and come back to this book often as your career grows!

Keywords

personal development; personal transformation; leadership; motivation; business and workplace culture; careers; psychology; ethics; self-help; growth

Contents

Testimonials

"Early in my career, I asked a mentor to help me chart out the next five years of my career. I wish I had this book then. I learned on my own the value of hard work, humility, sharing success with others, empowerment, and teamwork, but I believe I would have gotten there faster and with less anxiety and stress with this book in hand."—**Dan Neary, Retired CEO, Mutual of Omaha**

"Imagine a coach delivering the hard-won wisdom of hundreds of folks' careers right when you need it—just as you start in the working world. That's this book."—**Melissa Swift, U.S. Transformation Leader, Mercer**

"Am I Doing This Right *is a brilliant playbook filled with stories, anecdotes, and practical advice that is a must read for leaders embarking on their professional career."*—**Darlene DeRosa, Consultant in Leadership Advisory Services, Spencer Stuart**

"Am I Doing This Right? *bridges the gap between college and career. Its large survey and array of smart tips will help put any young person on a path to professional accomplishment and personal fulfillment."*—**Daniel H. Pink, #1** *New York Times* **best-selling author of** *The Power of Regret, Drive, and a Whole New Mind*

"Am I Doing This Right *represents an extraordinary resource for executives in the first decade of their careers. It is filled with great wisdom and coaching from some of the best, most successful leaders. It's a must read!"*—**Jim Loehr, Renowned Performance Psychologist, and** *New York Times* **best-selling author**

"Intention is almost everything in life, this book will show you where to put your attention."—**Paul Axtel, Consultant and Author of** *Being Remarkable*

"There are many stages of career and life. This book will give you the tools to master them both."—**Chad Holdorf, VP Digital Product Adoption, Pendo**

"Am I Doing This Right? *is like the mentor we wished we all had when we started our first job. If you are early in your career, do yourself a favor and read this book!"*—**Jon Gordon, 12x best-selling author of *The Carpenter and Training Camp***

"Leadership doesn't have to be mysterious. Am I Doing This Right *shares the wisdom of hundreds of leaders and outlines a plan for anyone brave enough to step up and do the work."*—**Seth Godin, Author, *Linchpin***

"A must read for new professionals or anyone looking to make a change in their careers! Am I Doing This Right *offers practical and timely knowledge, researched by the experts in the field."*—**Dr. Marshall Goldsmith, Thinkers50 #1 Executive Coach and *New York Times* best-selling author of *Triggers, Mojo,* and *What Got You Here Won't Get You There***

"Your early career and work experiences are like early deposits into your retirement or savings accounts. They could be energy deflators OR they could be early deposits in the YOU account. Your net worth in future decades in all aspects of that concept could be huge because of the compounding effect. It is not destiny but development at work. Early experiences have the greatest potential for your continued growth. This book is a major investment in your future!"—**Richard Boyatzis, PhD, Distinguished University Professor, Case Western Reserve University, Coauthor of the international best seller, *Primal Leadership and the New Helping People Change***

"Timely, relevant, and authentic! Whether you are starting your career or just a bit stuck, this book gives inspiration and tools to move forward and be better!"—**David Horsager, CEO and Author, Trust EDGE**

"This book is like having the most knowledgeable mentor possible at your disposal at all times! We spend the early parts of our careers wondering if we are 'doing this right.' This book answers that question and guides the reader

toward not only success but fulfillment in their career."—**Susan (Finerty) Zelmanski, Author and Consultant,** *Mastering the Matrix—7 Essentials to Getting Things Done in Complex Organizations*

"The world of professional career advice is full of rules and answers from successful figures. Refreshingly, Tony Thelen and his colleagues have written a valuable book to make us think through four important questions—who am I? Where am I going? How do I get there? What can I learn along the way? There's no expiry date to these questions and we will come up with newer answers when we pose them at different stages and times. They also do not want us to answer them silently, alone but as a community by sharing our stories as the fourth voice. While everyone's journey may seem different and unique, we see intersection points when we read other stories and share our own; we see ourselves in other stories more than we may have thought before. Read. Reflect. Share. Learn."—**Venkat Venkatraman, Professor of Management and Department Chair, Boston University Questrom School of Business**

Foreword

As a former university professor and now as a full-time speaker, executive leadership coach, and author, I'm always telling my students and clients there are only two ways to learn: T&E or OPE. Trial and Error or Other People's Experience.

This book is all about OPE. In other words, you get to learn what works and doesn't work by learning from the trials and triumphs of others. You get to learn, firsthand, whether or not *Am I Doing This Right?* when it comes to your own life and career.

You see, the most successful people, professionally and personally, are keenly tuned into OPE. They know life is too short and the cost is too high to rely solely on T&E. They can't afford to keep on making mistakes, failing unnecessarily, and hope to get ahead when there are proven shortcuts to the life, career, and relationships they want. This book will give you dozens, if not hundreds, of OPE shortcuts that will change your future for the better. I know because I know the author.

Tony Thelen and I met about a dozen years ago when he and his wife Sheila attended my two-day *Journey-to-the-Extraordinary* experience. It's an intense, highly interactive, hands-on boot camp designed to help the participants assess their lives and then set goals that will lead them to more positive and constructive lives. The participant reviews have always been over the top, but Tony was extraordinarily intent on applying everything he learned while at the *Journey*.

Immediately after the workshop, for example, Tony made goal setting and goal achievement the cornerstone of his life. He wrote out his annual goals, reviewed his progress every month, took notes, and kept track of everything that happened in the pursuit of his goals. He even reached out to people like me and several others to review his goals and goal achievement at the end of every year and get some coaching to help him move up to the next level.

As you can imagine, his results were over the top. Unprecedented success for Tony, on and off the job. He filled 10 binders, writing out the steps he had taken, the lessons he had learned, and the goal-setting system he had perfected.

Of course, I didn't know any of that was happening until a couple of years into the process. That's when Tony invited me to speak at some John Deere meetings, and we had a chance to talk about how the *Journey* affected him and how he was using it. He showed me his goal-setting system and his detailed notes. I was blown away. I immediately suggested that he consider putting his system into a book, because I knew the system was working for him and I knew it would work for others as well.

In 2020, Tony reached out to me again. He was ready to write this book and wanted some of my input. Of course, I was and am honored to help, especially so when I began to read his early drafts and realize the treasure his book would be for so many people.

Am I Doing This Right? takes a new and fresh approach that I have not seen anywhere else. It combines Tony's down-to-earth insights (some of which he learned from T&E) as a leader in business, with academically sound leading practices, and the voices of leaders from around the world. The result is a book that speaks to your head, touches your heart, taps into the T&E of other leaders, and gives you the fast-track OPE for your own highly successful fast-track for your own career and life.

Having spoken to and worked with hundreds of organizations and thousands of people, I keep on hearing the same refrain from my clients. They say such things as,

> I don't care about the theory or the buzz words of the day… I just want to know what works… I want to hit the ground running… I want to be happy and I want to be successful, but I'm not getting what I need from my school or classes… Help!

Perhaps you've felt some of that as well. You've taken a lot of classes, read a lot of books, attended various schools, and still feel like you're not prepared to thrive in the new world of work. Perhaps you've learned all kinds of "interesting facts," but you're still unsure of exactly "what you've got to do" and "how to do it" to ensure your own personal happiness and professional success.

Well, let me assure you this book provides many of the answers you're looking for. In a world flooded with good and not-so-good advice, I find this book invigorating because it moves beyond head knowledge and focuses on 18 key areas to be successful when you begin a new career or job. *Am I Doing This Right?* gives the right advice, at the right time, from the voices of experience, to help you realize your goals.

—Dr. Alan Zimmerman

March 2022

Author of *PIVOT: How One Turn In Attitude Can Lead to Success*

www.DrZimmerman.com

Acknowledgments

We would like to offer our sincere appreciation to the community of supporters who continue to ask, *am I doing this right?*

- To everyone who sent their stories to us in response to our survey questions—truly your stories were the fuel that inspired us to stay at it and bring this book to fruition. Supporting staff with Dedoose, Graphics, Reviewers, Editors, Publisher, and the over 1,000 people who contributed their stories during our research.

To those individuals who helped us along the way…

- To the people who poured into our careers too many to name!
- Sheila Thelen: Tireless advocate, expert in patience and proofreading, and helped design the original career experience survey used in our research.
- Mitchell family: For patience, support and forgiveness for dad and author.
- Alan Zimmerman: For being a great mentor to us in this process.
- Nathan Johnson: For providing that initial spark and encouragement.
- David Horsager: Motivator and trusted counsel.
- Susan (Finerty) Zelmanski: Best writing coach any author could ask for.
- Dan Roberts: Great advisor to help navigate this complex journey.
- Chrissy Culek: Research, data, and project management extraordinaire.
- Maggie Piotraschke: For bringing our intellectual ideas to the page.

- Vilma Barr and Scott Isenberg: Thank you for all the support.
- Becky Robinson: For helping us Reach! for all our goals.
- To all the reviewers, students, friends, family and colleagues who provided thoughtful feedback—this book is a reflection of your kindness and insight!

Author's Introduction

I have always been interested in learning new things. As a ten-year-old kid I used to listen to stories about college from my older brother. He was a biology major at Iowa State University, and I read all his textbooks. I used to capture and tag birds in my neighborhood and track their behavior in a notebook just like Marlon Perkins did on Mutual of Omaha's Wild Kingdom television show. While studying chemical engineering, I took a child psychology class to learn how the human mind evolved. When I was 42 years old, I took a night class on Anthropology while leading a software organization just to learn more about how humans evolved. For as long as I can remember, I have always been fascinated by learning about our world and personal growth.

I carried this love of learning into adulthood and every decade I try to take on a major learning activity. First was chemical engineering in college, then ten years after that it was an MBA, and 13 years after that it was a Post-Graduate Diploma in Strategy and Innovation from Oxford University. As the global pandemic started to bear down on the world in February 2020, it only seemed natural that I decide to get a PhD and write a leadership book.

I started to investigate what it would take to earn a PhD, I met with several professors from around the country who explained the process to me. They helped me discern not only what I would gain from the experience but also the substantial amount of time and resources I would need to dedicate to the effort. They helped me think through the opportunity cost of doing other things to learn versus the rigors needed to earn a doctoral degree. In the end it was not to be, but the process I went through ended up paying dividends in ways I could not have imagined.

The project of writing a book started with my writing letters to three authors whose books I had read. My simple request was to ask them to serve as my writing coach. Two immediately responded and enthusiastically agreed to help me. Second, I started a public, online survey to gauge others' interest telling the stories of their own careers.

The response I received was simply overwhelming both in the number of responses and in the depth and sincerity of the experiences described. People wrote about the most impactful events of their lives. They shared who gave them their greatest advice about moments of truth in their careers. They revealed what truly mattered in their careers.

In reading through these responses, I discovered people really wanted to tell their stories.

As my motivation from reading these stories skyrocketed, the project of writing the book itself began to take shape in an unusual way. During my PhD research, I met two professors from Drake University in Des Moines, Iowa, who became very interested in my project. As I outlined my concept of writing a leadership book based on my personal experience combined with the experience of others, their interest deepened. Over the course of 2020, a partnership formed with Matthew and Jeff to take the book project to the next level. Over the course of several meetings, we arrived at an aligned, shared objective, established mutual goals, and drafted a proposal that ultimately led to our writing this book.

While the goal of attaining a doctoral degree did not come to fruition, it was the process of discerning that goal ultimately led me to my coauthors. I believe meeting Matthew and Jeff was meant to happen and I believe this book was meant to be written.

Our main goal is simple: to help people *lead successful careers* and *live more fulfilling lives.*

I hope you enjoy reading this book and will use it as an inspirational guide to take action that will dramatically impact your life in a positive and constructive way. We also encourage you to share your own experiences with others! For more information on how to share your story, please visit the website: www.doingthisrightbooks.com. If you have a question, use the hashtag *#AmIDoingThisRight* on social media to solicit replies from our learning community. And let us celebrate your triumphs with you by using *#IAmDoingThisRight.*

Remember, we're all in this together!

—Tony Thelen
March 2022

Why Did We Write This Book?

This book is designed to help you build the foundation for a successful career and a fulfilling life in the first 10 years of your career. During the early stages of a career, and really throughout our lives, we believe it is normal and healthy to ask, *Am I Doing this Right?* One of the best investments of your time is to learn from the experience of others. We believe you can use the experience, insights, and lessons others have provided for this book to accelerate your own learning and development.

The aim of this book is to channel energy toward creating your future by giving you advice, tools, and the confidence to grow. Most importantly, we also believe you don't have to sacrifice a meaningful life to have a successful career: In fact, those two goals are *complementary, not conflicting.* That single lesson emerges powerfully through every hard-earned experience described within these pages as professionals examine how they have integrated their professional pursuits and personal victories.

Our ambition is that this book will serve as a "personal career desk reference" throughout the transitional time between school and professional life and then into the first years of your career. We hope you refer to these timeless lessons frequently because how you interpret their messages will change over time as your experiences evolve.

As such, take notes in the margins, revisit the chapters, take more notes, and someday hand this book down to others to share your story with them. As you read through the chapters, your voice and your story matter, and as such, we provide prompts for you to jot down insights, goals, and observations that will help you along the way.

While this book draws upon the stories and insights of others, at the end of the day it is a deeply personal book written for you and your life's story. With that in mind, consider transforming this this book into a journal with your own thoughts, stories, notes, and suggestions. In some ways, we actually believe this book is only half-written; to complete it, you need to *add your story*!

Book Design and Structure

This book focuses on areas of personal growth in the early stages of your career. When we began our research, we created a very simple survey asking for input from people around the world. The intent was to hear from others about the most important advice they had received and what were the most influential lessons they had learned. We asked questions like:

- What was the best advice you received in your career, and at what time during your career did you receive it (early, mid, late career)?
- What was the best career development tool/aid you found in your career? (e.g., a book, a degree, classroom experience, on-the-job training, etc.)
- What was the biggest problem you ever faced in your career, and how did you resolve it?

- Looking back, would you change anything as far as your career decisions are concerned? If so, what would you have changed and why?

We were overwhelmed by the response. We received amazing and thoughtful replies from over 1,000 leaders all over the world, in all kinds of professions, who wanted to share their hard-earned advice and tell their stories.

We poured over the data and identified dozens of attributes dealing with nearly every aspect of a successful career and fulfilling life. Most people told us the best advice they ever received came early in their career. Like compound interest, receiving great advice early in your life leads to compounding value throughout your professional life. As a result, we began to ask ourselves what was most important to study, learn, and experience *early in a career*? The answer to this question became the 18 chapters of this book. We have organized the chapters into four sections:

- Who am I?
- Where am I going?
- How do I get there?
- What can I learn along the way?

After sharing an early draft of the book, several reviewers pointed out the critical importance of understanding personal finance early in life and its implications for long-term success. As a result, we added a bonus chapter on financial acumen.

Who Is Speaking?

Think of this book as a literary orchestra with many musicians collaborating to create a work of art. In this spirit, there are four very important "contributors" to this book working in concert, each providing distinct and meaningful perspectives. They are:

- Tony Thelen, who draws upon his 34-year career to share personal experiences and lessons learned.

- Matthew Mitchell and Jeffrey Kappen who bring a wealth of experience from teaching and advising students at Drake University and from their strategy consulting and coaching practice at Bâton Global.
- Shared Words of Wisdom comprised of the stories and insights from hundreds of leaders around the world that provide a broad and deep wealth of experiences and counsel.

So, who is the last contributor? *That person is YOU.* The act of reading this book is very important. Equally vital is your own reflection. Take the time to collect personal insights and think about your experiences. Finally, it is critical that you become our coauthor and *take action* to develop your life and career with intention. #BiasTowardAction

Most of this book, apart from the "Shared Wisdom" sections, is written in the first person to create a more personal, one-on-one, conversational tone with the reader. Each chapter starts with a quote to trigger new thinking and prepare you to focus on the topic of the chapter. After a brief introductory paragraph, each chapter has four sections that are designed to make you think deeply about the topic at hand.

1. **Tony's Lessons From Personal Experience**: Each chapter begins with one of Tony's personal stories and lessons learned. The intent of this section is to serve as a consistent narrative throughout the book from a deeply personal perspective. It should get you to think about the issues surrounding the topic of the chapter and reflect how this may impact you and your life.

2. **Leading Practices**: This section provides concepts, insights, and tools for greater understanding of the topic of the chapter. Matthew and Jeff draw upon their many years of personal and professional consulting and academic experience to help you more fully develop your understanding and skills. Compared to Tony's more personal stories, Matthew and Jeff take the reader directly into action with best practices.

3. **Shared Wisdom: Lessons From the Road**: Now that we have heard Tony's personal story and learned about some leading practices, the next section draws our attention to the experiences of others. What

can we learn from the most salient life lessons from others? How does this relate to your life? How can we use what others have learned during their career and integrate their experience to improve our situation? We've gleaned the best insights we received from others and provide them for your review and reference. This section serves two key purposes—to inform you on what others have said was most important in their career, and, secondly, to serve as a reference group of professionals who have struggled with the same issues you do. You are joining a community, a process, and a tradition that extends well beyond any one person's life.

4. **Reflections: What's Your Story?**: Finally, each chapter concludes with a direct appeal for you to focus on *your story*. You've read Tony's story, you've reviewed Matthew and Jeff's leading practices, you've reflected upon the insights from others, now it's time to really get down to business and determine what relevance it all has for you. This section contains reflection questions for deeper meaning and understanding with space to jot down your thoughts. We will ask you to relate the topic to your own experience thus far and at times "nudge" you to act and do something differently in your life. Here is where you become our "coauthor" and make the most out of this book. We highly recommend pausing and reflecting to record your thoughts and then taking time to revisit them as your career progresses.

5. **Going Further: Questions, Readings and References**: For those of you who want just a little more on the topic of each chapter, check out this section for great discussion questions, suggested readings, and chapter references we have found useful.

It's important to note that as your life changes, and your priorities and circumstances evolve, the topics of each chapter may take on greater or lesser significance. With this in mind, you may want to read through this book from start to finish, or you may jump to a particular chapter that is highly relevant to your current situation. Either approach works well as each of the book's chapters is designed to stand on its own.

No matter how you decide to read this book, we recommend that you always keep it handy and refer to the chapters as your thinking and maturity evolve and life experiences change. Revisiting a given chapter a year or more after first reading it may lead to deeper, more personal insights. Remember, our goal is to become the best version of ourselves. President Theodore Roosevelt once remarked in a speech that "Comparison is the thief of joy!" so celebrate your own progress without becoming too distracted by others'. Your story is unique, and the experiences and journey of your life are like no other. While we recognize that our writing is certainly informed by our own backgrounds and experiences, it is our ultimate hope that you use this book to shape your path forward in the pursuit of professional success and a fulfilling life. Let the journey begin!

PART 1

Who Am I?

Self-Image, Personal Brand, Balance, and Well-Being

CHAPTER 1

Self-Image

SELF-IMAGE
SELF-AWARENESS
PERSPECTIVES
FAMILY
COMMUNITY

Some day when I get all the tools hung up in my own garage maybe someone will find out that it's not such a screwed-up shop after all.
—Tony Thelen, Author
Personal Journal, November 11, 1987 (20 years old)

Introduction

Before we can look at what we might accomplish in the world, we have to come to terms with how we view ourselves. When we establish a healthy self-image, we can then develop healthy relationships with others. We can interpret the rest of the world coming from a place of acceptance and strength. Pitfalls such as imposter syndrome, lack of confidence, and not understanding your true value may all become hardened in our lives without a healthy self-image.

As your life unfolds, you will face more and more complex issues. A positive self-image will enable you to deal with these changes in positive and constructive ways. This chapter underscores the importance of caring for your self-image while providing you tools and advice to help you get started right.

Tony's Lessons From Personal Experience

For most of my life, I've measured my value based on what others thought. Parents, older siblings, friends, teachers, professors, bosses, colleagues, my wife, and my own children have all impacted my self-image. Specifically, seeking external affirmation and approval has driven me and my self-image. It still influences me and my attitude daily to some degree.

There is no doubt external approval has driven me and provided fuel for my ambitions. However, it has also placed me on a treadmill that never seems to end. It has caused a thirst in me that can never quite be quenched. On the one hand, that's a good thing that it continues to motivate me in a healthy way to be conscious of my behavior, performance, or ambition. On the other hand, I am sure it has limited my success and happiness in times when I have fallen short of a task or activity. The sword cuts both ways so to speak.

All the same, when I have failed or somehow fallen short in my life, I tend to be hard on myself. I've been nicked by experiences that seem to be etched in my memory. Some memories just stay with you forever. For example, I failed the first test I ever took in college and had to drop the class. I missed the first Thanksgiving dinner at my future in-laws because I lost track of time deer hunting with my brother. My first presentation in a professional setting earned me a spot in a presentation skills class and a suggestion that I join Toastmasters International. Let's just say I wasn't exactly great at first impressions.

At times over my career, I have been slow to own a problem, slow to respond to an evolving issue, and at times completely missed the mark on a critical project. These only start to scratch the surface where I have let myself and others down throughout my life. *Even just reliving these events is a downer!*

What I have learned most about my self-image over the years is how to think about both the external and internal factors differently. I've learned to soften the influence of the external and only use it when it helps me find the fuel to motivate me in some way. I've learned to cultivate the intrinsic, to be at peace with myself, to be at peace with the universe, and know that while I walk in a world full of expectations, it is OK, and I am OK, if I show up and do my best. I am focused on becoming the best version of myself. I am not focused on endless self-judgment of myself in comparison to others.

In the end, I have learned that most of the time I am good enough. While there is no doubt my shortcomings have and always will inform my psyche, they don't have a complete monopoly on how I view myself. I've realized that in the end, I am in control of how I feel about my life and how I feel about myself. *I have choices* about how I view my self-image.

A special note about social media. Social media can have a devastating effect on you if you let it, especially younger kids but even as adults we are susceptible to keeping up appearances on social media. My advice? Be careful with social media and make sure to only use it to help make life better for you and do your best to avoid getting caught up in other people's opinions and all the negativities.

It's critical to find a way that works for you to maintain a healthy self-image. Find the good in any issue or situation, and move forward, informed, always onward and upward regardless of whether you realize success or disappointment. In the beginning, in the end, and at any point in between, you are in control of how you feel and how you choose to interpret the world around you.

No matter where you are in life, having a positive self-image is important to get the most out of life. It's a conversation that will never end, a story that will always have another chapter, in a life that opens every day with an opportunity to be better than the day before.

Leading Practices

Current research suggests that *self-image* is one part of a broader theory of self-concept (Ackerman 2021); that also includes self-esteem, self-efficacy, and self-awareness. At its core, self-image is how an individual sees themselves. It is the mental picture of oneself that is formed through collected experiences, successes, failures, and may include simple physical attributes (tall, short, brunette, etc.) but also core values that have been learned over time (e.g., honesty, courage, loyalty, hard work, etc.). Below, we have outlined three leading practices to help understand and describe your self-image:

- Inside-Out: Knowing Your Self-Conception
- Outside-In: Knowing Others' Perspectives
- Genogram or Family Tree

Inside-Out: Who Am I?

To maintain a healthy self-image, you need at least two different perspectives: First, you need to cultivate *self-awareness* that allows you to consciously identify your own thoughts, feelings, behaviors, and values (Cherry 2020). Socrates is often quoted as saying that "To know thyself is the beginning of wisdom". This is what we call the inside-out view, and it is critically important to self-discovery.

The ancient Greek maxim, "Know Thyself," is inscribed upon the Temple of Apollo at Delphi

One way to explore your own self-image is to take the Twenty Statements Test (Kuhn and McPartland 1954). This simple assessment asks you to answer the question "Who am I?" 20 times. You can sort your answers into four main categories to understand your self-image (Rees and Nicholson 2004).

1. *Physical self:* Statements about physical characteristics such as age, home location, and so on. (e.g., I am tall.)
2. *Social self:* Identifications of the self in relation to social groupings (interpersonal) and norms. (e.g., I am a welder.)
3. *Reflective self:* Statements that make reference or imply a specific pattern of behavior such as attitudes, values, and needs. (e.g., I am very self-confident.)

4. *Oceanic self*: Self-identifications that are vague, abstract, or fail to differentiate themselves from anyone else. (e.g., I am made of stardust.)

TWENTY STATEMENTS TEST
Self-Image psychological profile

There are twenty numbered blanks on the page below. Please write twenty answers to the simple question "Who Am I?" in the blanks. Answer as if you were giving the answers to yourself, not somebody else. Write the answers in the order that they occur to you. Don't worry about logic or "importance". Go along fairly fast.

1. _____
2. _____
3. _____
4. _____
5. _____
6. _____
7. _____
8. _____
9. _____
10. _____
11. _____
12. _____
13. _____
14. _____
15. _____
16. _____
17. _____
18. _____
19. _____
20. _____

Knowing how you construct your individual identity can be incredibly helpful as you relate with others and the world around you. This simple Twenty Statements Test is powerful, but there are many other assessments that can help you understand more about yourself (e.g., Five Factor Model, Hogan Assessment, Birkman, and Predictive Index). Interestingly, recent research has found that none of these are 100 percent accurate and they can also be counterproductive if they "label" you permanently or suggest you cannot ever change (Meinert 2015). We have used some of these tests to open a conversation, but please remember you should always interpret the results carefully and remember they are not definitive.

Outside-In: Knowing Others' Perspectives

Second, you also need to reach out to solicit others' perspectives from time to time. Getting feedback from others complements your inside-out self-awareness to complete a full picture of who you really are.

Formal 360-degree reviews are the most formalized method of soliciting other perspectives. 360-degree reviews involve asking your leader(s), your peers, and your direct reports to provide feedback on your development. These are used for formal performance reviews, but it doesn't need to be that complicated. Simply remaining curious and welcoming additional perspectives is an immensely useful practice that can benefit any aspiring leader. For example, at the end of each meeting, you can ask for feedback about your performance or contribution on a scale of 1 to 10. Or you can develop trusting relationships with peers or leaders who are willing to share their observations about your development over time. Specific recommendations to get the best developmental feedback include:

- *Ask for Specifics*: It can be difficult but asking for specifics will focus your attention.
- *Don't Wait, Ask Now*: It can be easy to wait until that perfect time. The truth is, there is no better time than the present.
- *Be Grateful*: Say "Thank You" and withhold judgment before responding.
- *Monitor Your Mood*: Don't ask for feedback when you're hangry!
- *Role Model*: If you're going to ask for constructive feedback, also be willing to offer it.
- *Follow Through*: If you receive useful feedback, be sure to act on it!

This balance of "inside-out" and "outside-in" perspectives will help you construct a more holistic and accurate self-image. By remaining curious, you can own, influence, and actively shape that self-image over time in a way that aligns with your long-term goals!

Genogram or Family Tree

For many of us, our family relationships are the framework upon which our life is constructed. We grow up with certain traditions, foods, quirks, or family stories. These family experiences all come together to help shape how we learn about ourselves and ultimately help inform who we become. Some of these family traits are very helpful while others may be more challenging or damaging.

A genogram is tool used to represent those key family elements that could shape our self-image. Formally defined by the American Psychological Association (APA), a genogram is:

> A diagrammatic representation of a family that includes pedigree information—that is, individual histories of illness and death—but also incorporates aspects of the interpersonal relationships between family members.

For our purposes, genograms or family trees can help us understand ourselves better by focusing on our relationships with our family and how that has shaped our own view of the world. There are many resources online to create a professional genogram or family tree, but these following simple steps will help get you started:

- Collect some of your basic family information—maybe speak with your parents or relatives to learn some of their stories and influences.
- Draw out your basic family tree to the best of your ability, leaving space for more descriptive details/reflection if possible.
- For each person, describe the dominant elements of their personality and how it affected you (e.g., my grandmother was a great baker... and her attention to detail inspired me).
- After you've completed a rough first draft, then reflect upon how the elements of your family have or have not influenced you. Do you see any themes? Is there anything you hope to maintain? Is there anything you would like to consciously leave behind?

Finally, while we are all influenced by our past, it is most important to note that you are not only the sum-total of your familial experiences. You control your own life. Being aware of which elements of your past can help shape your understanding of the present and support achieving your goals for the future.

Shared Wisdom: Lessons From the Road

When our community of leaders were asked to think about their leadership journeys, many issues relating to self-image were brought to the surface. Attitude, ownership, comparing yourself to others, and feelings of inferiority or being an imposter all loomed large.

Below Darrell shares how important the pursuit of self-awareness and authenticity is to him, and how it relates to his viewing himself as a servant leader.

I believe in four fundamentals to lead well. I have to pursue two things every day: (1) Self-awareness; (2) Authenticity. I have to do two things every day: (3) Inspire; (4) Influence. Learning humility and a servant attitude enables these four. It is a daily pursuit.

—Darrell Pankratz, Executive Chairman
AgriVision and Prairieland Partners John Deere dealerships,
Kansas, USA

A founder of a tech startup in London shares the influence an early senior manager had on her career and how this aided her in elevating her self-image.

Early in my career, one of my senior managers gave me the visibility and tools to grow in the company, professionally in general, and as a person. She said, "I want you to fly." It was the best empowering message a leader could have given me in my early days, it helped me understand what type of professional and leader I wanted to be.

—Founder of a tech startup
Sustainable technology industry, London, England

A vice president in the software industry shares how important your attitude is early in your career and how critical it is to view yourself in a positive light.

The attitude is a push factor to success. If you think yourself a small potato, you will behave like a junior staff, no matter how many years in your career; If you think yourself a CEO (doing things wholeheartedly), your behavior will be responsible and people will feel it. I experienced it 15 years after I graduated.

—Vice President
Software industry, Iowa, USA

Shawn, owner of a consulting firm, shares his experience on self-esteem and how important it is to come from within.

Early in my career I learned that self-esteem comes from within yourself. I know this is simple and straight-forward, but I had been having a lot of people control my confidence in my work. My manager helped me realize that confidence was within my power, and I had more control than I realized.

—Shawn A. Noble, PhD, President
Noble Consulting Group, North Carolina, USA

Tavonga, a technology leader at Google, explains how during a time of doubt the personal focus on always getting better produced the confidence he needed to continue to grow in his career.

Strive to be the best version of yourself. I received this advice a few years into my career (~5 years), during a time of doubt as to whether I had the ingredients to grow into the company leader I aspired to become—and not fully appreciating the beautiful uniqueness we all bring.

—Tavonga Siyavora, Partnerships
Google X, California, USA

Molly, a director in supply management, shares how vital it is to *"be you."* She realized the full impact that listening to other people's feedback had on her confidence, happiness, and uniqueness. Her experience also illustrates the importance of timing: sometimes we are more open to advice while other times we may be closed even to receiving good counsel.

Be You, the World Needs It! After 20 years with the company where I assumed I would retire, I was nominated to be part of a Women's Leadership program—I was ecstatic for the opportunity and vowed to make the most of it. Through that program, I met so many amazing women, but one in particular suggested I meet with an astrologer who shared this advice with me after a reading. The words are simple, but the timing of them was profound for me and helped me see that I had listened too much to all of the feedback I'd been given in my career. The problem with much of the feedback was that it essentially erased what made me unique. Over 20 years I slowly covered up what differentiated myself from the crowd and led to my inability to make the impact I wanted in my life and career. It also made me blame myself for not being enough which further eroded my confidence and my happiness.

—Molly Krueger, Director of Global Sourcing
Renewable Energy Group, Iowa, USA

Haley, who transitioned to a fractional chief marketing officer after a very successful marketing and product leadership career for a major biotech company, shares the wisdom of listening to your inner voice.

I would have found my voice sooner and been more the hero of my own story. I would have also coached my younger self to relax a little and not worry so much about the small stuff or other people's opinions of you.

—Haley Stomp, Fractional Chief Marketing Officer
Biotech, Iowa, USA

A strategy consultant at a major global consulting firm shares the challenges of starting her career as a black woman and overcoming imposter syndrome.

Feeling like an imposter. As a young black woman in industries that primarily do not look like me, I used to struggle all the time. My resolution? Finding commonalities with colleagues and clients. Connecting with them on a more personal level and allowing them to get to know me. You'd be surprised how much more enjoyable it is to work with people who you know personally and feel like they know you as well. How could I be an imposter in my own world of knowing people and them knowing me? I couldn't.

—Strategy Consultant
Global Consulting, Illinois, USA

Similarly, Jenny, owner of her own consulting firm, shares the value of learning to overcome imposter syndrome as one of the most important lessons she learned.

The concept of the Imposter Syndrome i.e., that I don't believe I'm good enough, but I am! I heard this as part of a leadership program seven years into my career.

—Jenny Schmidt, President
J. Schmidt Consulting, Iowa, USA

Bill, an executive coach and former CEO and chairman of an aviation services firm, shares his experience of his fear of failure that led to his feelings of being an imposter, only to find that taking action led to greater career growth and more fulfilling connection with his organization.

Overcoming fear of failure following a string of rapid promotions. I learned that "imposter syndrome" is a very real thing. I felt so disconnected and uninformed in a new leadership role. After about a week of "faking it," I decided to undertake a two-week boot camp style training regimen, working in entry-level positions, meeting customers, and working my way around the organization. I rapidly gained comfort and confidence, deeper understanding, and connected with great people.

—Bill Koch, Executive Coach,
Koch Leadership, Texas, USA

Finally, Sara, a software engineering manager, shares her advice on building confidence early in her career and how important it is to have a positive view of yourself when looking at your potential as a leader.

I would learn about gender differences and confidence in females so that I wouldn't question myself so much. I would learn more about other people's failures to realize it happens and boosts careers in better directions. I would not have tried to keep my ego so low when I became a manager. I kept it so small that I shrunk myself. I've learned that who you're made to be can't shine if you make yourself too small.
—Sara Van Wyngarden, Software Engineering Manager
PushPay, Colorado, USA

You are what you are, and you are where you are, because of what has gone into your mind. You change what you are and you change where you are by changing what goes into your mind.
—Zig Ziglar, Author
See You at the Top

Reflections: What's Your Story?

1. What are your main insights/takeaways from the chapter at this moment?

_____

_____

_____

_____

_____

_____

_____

_____

_____

2. What are one to three goals/intentions you would like to set for yourself?

_____

_____

_____

_____

_____

_____

_____

_____

_____

Going Further: Questions, Readings, and References

Discussion Questions

1.1   Tony talked about how his self-image was influenced by external factors such as people in his life—what external factors influence your self-image the most?

1.2   Several of our leaders commented on "imposter" syndrome. Have you ever felt like an imposter and if so, what did you do to move forward despite it?

1.3   Make a list of 5 or 10 things you did right over the last 30 to 60 days. How did you feel writing these things down? Do the same for 5 or 10 things that didn't go so well. How does your attitude change after writing these down?

1.4   In the leading practices, Matthew and Jeffrey outline the Twenty Questions Test. Take a moment to do this and reflect on the four categories of self (Physical, Social, Reflective, and Oceanic). Did anything surprise you about the results?

1.5   Think back to times when you have been criticized for something. How did that make you feel at the time, and how did this influence your self-image?

1.6   How would you currently describe your self-image today? Has this changed over time?

Suggested Reading

Brown, B. 2021. *Atlas of the Heart: Mapping Meaningful Connection and the Language of Human Experience*. Random House.

Hardy, D. 2010. *The Compound Effect: Jumpstart Your Income, Your Life, Your Success*. New York, NY: Hachette.

Ziglar, Z. 1974. *See You at the Top*. New Orleans, LA: Pelican Publishing.

Zimmerman, A. 2006. *Pivot*. Austin, TX: Greenleaf Group Book Press.

References

Ackerman, C.E. 2021. "What Is Self-Concept Theory? A Psychologist Explains." *Positive Psychology*. https://positivepsychology.com/self-concept/

Cherry, K. 2020. "What Is Self-Awareness? Very Well Mind." *Verywell Mind.* www.verywellmind.com/what-is-self-awareness-2795023

Kuhn, M.H., and T.S. McPartland. 1954. "An Empirical Investigation of Self-Attitudes." *American Sociological Review* 19, no. 1, pp. 68–76. https://doi.org/10.2307/2088175

Meinert, D. 2015. "What Do Personality Tests Really Reveal?" SHRM. www.shrm.org/hr-today/news/hr-magazine/pages/0615-personality-tests.aspx

Rees, A., and N. Nicholson. 2004. "The Twenty Statements Test." In *Qualitative Methods in Organizational Research: A Practical Guide*, eds. C. Cassell and G. Symon, pp. 86–97. London: Sage.

CHAPTER 2

Personal Brand

PERSONAL
BRAND

LABELS
SELF-REFLECTION
AUTHENTICITY

Don't let the noise of other people's opinions drown out your inner voice.

—Steve Jobs, Cofounder, Chairman, and CEO
Apple and Pixar, California, USA
2005 Stanford Commencement Address

Introduction

Personal brand focuses on others' perspectives of who you are. When someone interacts with you, even for a relatively short period of time, they develop an image of who you are. Parents, friends, coworkers, family members, and neighbors will all have different perspectives of who you are based on how long they have known you and their experiences with you.

Being aware of your personal brand and cultivating it at an early stage will enable you to influence and shape how others experience your presence and perceive your leadership. It is important to stay aware to how this may change over time as well. As you take on more responsibilities, so must you adapt to how you show up each day. Be mindful that every interaction represents an opportunity to be intentional about your personal and professional brand. Literally every day you have an opportunity to be the best possible version of yourself, improve on who you were the day before, and build your personal brand in a positive way.

This chapter provides some guidelines and exercises to help you cultivate and build a positive relationship with your personal brand and gives you a strong starting point for a lifetime of growth.

Tony's Lessons From Personal Experience

Labels can make a difference on how others judge you. When I did well on a math test in third grade, I remember being asked to take a timed math test against the school principal. Ever since that day, I was labeled a math whiz. When I decided to study chemical engineering, I noticed some people treated me differently even though I didn't feel that much different. When I got a job with John Deere, I noticed a change in how people perceived me.

I didn't know it at the time, but my personal brand was evolving. It continued when I got married, when I had a family, when I got promoted, and when I went back to school for graduate studies at the University of Northern Iowa and Oxford University.

On the downside I've had more than a few experiences where I can say my personal brand was negatively impacted as well. Like when I got seven speeding tickets in one year from the Kansas State Patrol. Or when I backed my father-in-law's car into a fire hydrant. As a kid growing up, I wanting to be like the famous mountain man Jim Bridger or the frontiersman Daniel Boone. When I was ten years old, the bird population in my neighborhood precipitously dropped after I got my first BB gun. One of the parents on the block called the police and they caught me in the act with a pile of dead birds in the alley behind our home. As part of my punishment, the police department made me write a 1,000-word essay on the value of songbirds in society. I tend not to dwell on these too deeply but no doubt my personal brand was impacted.

Everything counts, and all your experiences and interactions influence how the outside world views you.

All of my life experiences have certainly shaped my personal brand. At the same time, none of these experiences on their own completely defines who I am. At best, they are but one part of the multifaceted person I am. There is so much more to me than meets the eye (and I imagine there is so much more to you as well)! I am often reminded of the personal growth and potential I have yet to discover. Sometimes I do the discovering, and other times it takes someone else to believe in me. Sometimes others need to push me a little to help me to see what I'm capable of.

A personal brand is influenced by your interactions with others and the decisions you make in your life. I know that I have a professional image to live up to at work. That is different than who I am at home with my family and personal friends. I also have a public identity others see: my resume on LinkedIn, my last update to Instagram or Facebook, or my latest post to Twitter. Context matters to me when I think about my personal brand. I don't think this means being two-faced or living an inconsistent life, or not having integrity or anything like that. It just means that when I am in a professional setting, I act like it, and when I am in a personal setting, I can be more personal in my behavior. It means I try to be savvy with whatever circumstances I find myself in and I try to be aware and intentional and smart about how I behave in different situations.

Perhaps most important to me is to appreciate the parts of my personal brand I care about most. To me, for example, they include being a Believer, a Husband, a Father, a Son, a Brother, a Friend, a Colleague, a Coach, a Mentor, a Teammate, and a Student of Life.

One of my core beliefs is that I am 100 percent responsible for my life no matter where I am and the circumstances I am dealing with. Whatever decisions I made in my past brought me to where I am every moment of my life. In the end, maybe my best personal brand advice is simply to be yourself no matter the circumstances. I try to authentically be the person

I need to be in order to honor the moment and the people I am around. Therein may lie my highest good, my most human of all brands, to be myself and true to my values every moment of my life.

Leading Practices

Cultivating a consistent, personal brand can help you stand out for opportunities when people meet you, follow your social media, and screen your background. It indicates to people what you stand for and communicates how your life's narrative comes together in a coherent fashion. Having a consistent, honest message will inspire trust, set expectations, and set the stage for authentic relationships.

- Why a Personal Brand is Important
- Crafting a Personal Brand Statement
- Managing Your Brand over Time

Why a Personal Brand Is Important

What is so important about identity? An identity is important to operate socially or in a professional environment. Your identity is a social guide that conveys respect, rapport, or common interest. When parents meet, they may tell stories about raising kids. When people who love fishing meet, they talk about the lakes and rivers they've seen or on the biggest one that got away. People who grew up in the same state or country will quickly pivot to their shared past and traditions. Having a positive shared identity can help people relate to others more quickly and closely, thereby forming stronger bonds over time through common experiences.

It is likely that people will only know a version of you, a somewhat public persona perceived through a lens in a professional world where many people can't or don't take/make the time to notice the full person. This is rightly so as we all have limited resources, and we should not judge, but at the same time, we need to understand that the best way to care for our identities is through self-reflection and the inner discovery of who we really are, what we are truly capable of doing, and what mark we wish to leave upon the world.

Research and interest in identity has yielded a robust literature examining how individual and social identities are created and maintained. To cover this entire history is far too vast for this chapter, so the focus here will be cultivating your professional identity.

There are three recognized processes in this area, including (a) self-labeling as a professional, (b) integration of skills and attitudes considered appropriate for that career, and (c) a perception of being a member of a professional community.

As you begin your career, this means you need to recognize the outside expectations of the path you have chosen to follow. For some careers, where education and licensing requirements are clearly set out, this may be relatively straightforward at first. Regardless, as you enter, what you do with those initial skills is up to you. Networking with others, engagement in public forums, pursing experiences to build your career, and serving in leadership roles will all help bolster your professional identity over time.

Crafting Your Personal Brand

Developed by Dave Ulrich and Norm Smallwood (2007), this exercise challenges you to state succinctly who you want to be and why. Some people will craft a few phrases for different contexts for example, work, family life, and so on. The basic personal brand formula is simply:

I want to be known for _____, so that I can deliver _____.

For example:

- I want to be known for being innovative so that I can deliver new solutions to client problems.
- I want to be known for being empathetic so that I can help friends and neighbors in need.

Taking the time to reflect on your own legacy (or what you want to be known for) and the impact you want to have on others (i.e., your value proposition) gives you a measuring stick against which to weigh your own choices and behaviors. It may also allow you to say no to options that are inconsistent or will take too much energy away from outcomes you have identified as the most important. Monitor and iterate on your brand. There are additional exercises in *Purpose* (Chapter 5) which may help you think about how to develop your brand in line with your purpose and values.

Managing Your Personal Brand

Having an authentic brand reinforces the importance of self-reflection and careful decision making. Whatever you decide to do, you should do it well. Be sincere in pursuing your passions and making the choices that will shape your identity and career in ways that align to your values and your integrity. If the path is not the right one, or if you take a small wrong turn, take action to reorient and rebuild. In the 21st century, as many people repeatedly change careers and companies, there is ample room for correction if you find yourself yearning for reinvention.

One place to begin managing your personal brand is to consider your own negative and positive self-talk when you are confronted with a situation that challenges you or your personal brand (see Positive Self-Talk resource from ReCap Australia below).

Situation	Negative self-talk	Positive self-talk
"Example: Speaking to someone new"	I'm dull. They won't want to talk to me.	"I'm interesting. Maybe I'll make a new friend."
Feelings	*Frightened*	*Excited*
1. Trying a new problem	I'll make a mistake.	The more I try the better I'll get.
Feelings		
2. Giving a talk to the class	They'll laugh and tease me.	I can do it.
Feelings		
3. Asking if you can join a game	They don't like me.	This will be fun.
Feelings		
4. Asking to borrow something special	They'll say no.	They'll say yes.
Feelings		
5. Giving an opinion	They'll all laugh.	They'll think I'm smart.
Feelings		
6. Making a speech	I'll make a fool of myself.	I'll do a pretty good job.
Feelings		

With time you will discover that reframing your reactions to situations will be very helpful to avoid spending too much energy on expecting (unlikely) tragedy or stressful anticipation of an undesirable outcome.

Shared Wisdom: Lessons From the Road

These quotes from people at all stages in their careers provide insight into how they have chosen to craft their own brands with an awareness of the importance of other's opinions and validations of who we are and may choose to become. We can all benefit from avoiding an automatic acceptance of labels others place on us without proper examination.

Jason, a global leader living in Singapore, shares the value of being yourself and bringing your full self to work.

> *Be who you are. It's a simple statement but when you really pick it apart there's a lot there. First, there's the obvious part, don't try to conform to everything and everyone around you. People can sometimes spend too much time trying to fit in and worrying about the politics and the optics of things. Some of that is, of course, necessary because we are a team and there are some norms established. However, if we are really trying to build an inclusive environment, it starts with leaders being authentic. Don't focus too much on trying to emulate others but do learn from them. Bring your full self to work. It's the only way to build a truly highly engaged team around you. And that team, not you, is what is going to make a difference long term.*
>
> —Jason P. H. Brantley, Director Asia, Africa, and Middle East
> John Deere, Singapore

Mark, owner of an engineering firm, shares the value he found in his personal brand by finding his purpose that led to years of personal growth.

> *My crisis came when I realized that I was miserable and absolutely frustrated with my career. I initially believed that I was deeply flawed, and I would never be able to be a productive member of a civilian team. I wrestled with the fact that I was not able to "not take it*

personally" and I had no interest in finding a "work/life balance" or
"leaving work at work." I also could not just accept poor management
and weak leadership as status quo. I tried several different jobs, but I
faced the same frustration and misery each time. But then I realized,
I was made for a purpose. All of my unique experiences were not proof
of failure but a unique journey that created a unique individual.
The qualities that I saw as a fatal flaw were actually highly rare and
valuable qualities, if they were used correctly. Eventually, I was able to
form a unique business case out of these leadership qualities.

—Mark Barglof, President and Owner
Kinetic Technologies, Iowa, USA

An information technology professional from Chicago shares how being aware of limitations led to the correct identification the skills and capabilities.

I have always been my biggest problem in my career. Being self-aware
is a continuous challenge along with finding/building the right skills
within my capabilities to work with and coach my team to achieve
the optimal results.

—Chief Information Security Officer
Technology industry, Illinois, USA

Kathy, a Chief Information Officer for a Fortune 250 company, shares the importance of owning your career and advocating for your personal brand.

Early in my career, a very senior leader said that I own my career. It
was impactful and I realized from then on that I needed to advocate
for myself.

—Kathy Kay, Chief Information Officer
Principal Financial Group, Iowa, USA

Raquel, a president of her own health and change management consulting firm, offers advice she received that helped her understand her personal brand during critical moments of her career.

Your job does not define who you are. Who you are defines the job you happen to have. I received several pieces of advice throughout my career (when I got laid off, when I was part of an acquisition) and I put those pieces together to create that summary.

—Dr. Raquel Garzon, President
Revitalize Project, New Mexico, USA

A regional manager from Tennessee shares the peace of mind that is gained by aiming to be yourself, know your strengths, and seek continuous improvement.

Be yourself. I received this advice at the beginning of my career when I was having a hard time connecting to my students as a business instructor. About 17 years later, I got the same advice after receiving several promotions and serving as a leader in my company. I finally accept that I'm not my best self when I try to fit a mold. I know my strengths, I accept my opportunities, and I look for ways to improve every day.

—Regional Manager
Automotive industry, Tennessee, USA

Reflections: What's Your Story?

1. What are your main insights/takeaways from the chapter at this moment?

_____

_____

_____

_____

_____

_____

_____

_____

_____

2. What are one to three goals/intentions you would like to set for yourself?

_____

_____

_____

_____

_____

_____

_____

_____

_____

_____

_____

_____

Going Further: Questions, Readings, and References

Discussion Questions

2.1 Tony talked about both positive and not so positive aspects of his personal brand. Take a moment and jot down every word that comes to mind when you think about your personal brand. Which are most important to you and which ones would you rather see go away over time?

2.2 Many leaders talk about the need to "be yourself" as part of your personal brand. When are you "yourself" the most, and when do you feel like you have to be someone else?

2.3 How have negative and positive self-talk impacted your personal brand?

2.4 When others think of you, what do you think they would say about you? How do you feel when you think about this?

2.5 What does it take for something to have an impact on your personal brand? What moments in life have impacted your personal brand the most, for example, decisions, events, people, and so on?

2.6 Have you ever been labeled something, and it stuck to your personal brand? Have you ever labeled someone else a particular way and it stuck? How might you think differently about how you view your personal brand in the future based on these experiences?

Suggested Reading

Goins, J. 2015. *The Art of Work: A Proven Path to Discovering What You Were Meant to Do*. Nashville, TN: Nelson Books.

Nuñez, G. 2018. *Take Charge of Your Brand: Quick and Simple Techniques to Help You Own and Manage Your Personal Brand for Professional and Personal Success*. Scotts Valley, CA; CreateSpace Publishing.

Rath, T. 2007. *StrengthsFinder 2.0*. Omaha, NE: Gallup Press.

References

Positive Self-Talk. 2004. ReCap–Recovery Capitals. Commonwealth of Australia.

Ulrich, D. and N. Smallwood. 2007. "Building a Leadership Brand." *Harvard Business Review* 85, no. 7–8, pp. 92–100.

CHAPTER 3

Balance

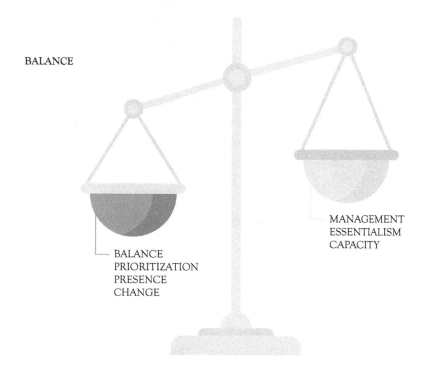

BALANCE

BALANCE
PRIORITIZATION
PRESENCE
CHANGE

MANAGEMENT
ESSENTIALISM
CAPACITY

Imagine life as a game in which you are juggling some five balls in the air. You name them—work, family, health, friends, and spirit—and you're keeping all of these in the air. You will soon understand that work is a rubber ball. If you drop it, it will bounce back. But the other four balls—family, health, friends, and spirit—are made of glass. If you drop one of these, they will be irrevocably scuffed, marked, nicked, damaged, or even shattered. They will never be the same. You must understand that and strive for balance in your life.

—Brian Dyson, CEO (Retired)
Coca Cola Enterprises, Georgia, USA

Introduction

Life is full of trade-offs. Reflecting on the previous quote, on the one hand, there are constant work demands; on the other hand, we need to consider nonwork related needs, desires, and obligations. What is most important to you? What priorities guide choices in your life? Establishing and maintaining proper perspective on how to balance the important aspects of your life is what this chapter is all about.

In the early stages of your career, it's relatively simple to focus on your performance at work. Some people will pour their lives into their jobs and make tremendous investments in the pursuit of professional success. But how might we approach balancing such effort with energy for the other multiple, equally important aspects of our lives? This chapter prompts reflection about the importance of ensuring that we allocate time and energy in alignment with all our priorities.

Tony's Lessons From Personal Experience

It seems we are handed an implied goal at some point in our career to keep everything in balance. Every component of our lives that we deem important should pull on us with equal demand for our time and energy. What constitutes these key compartments are typically things like work, family, hobbies, sports, spiritual practices, and personal wellness like exercise, eating, and sleeping. Just like the tires on our vehicles, most of us tend to only pay attention to balance in our lives most when we are "out of balance." Experiencing such stress or a lingering sense of discomfort may serve as an early warning system that our choices need to change.

I'll never forget the feeling of being seriously out of control in my career and the profound stress it created in my being. Today I can easily look back and say this helped me grow and develop who I am today, but at the time it felt like a strange mix between feeling truly lost without a map and a sense I couldn't control my destiny. If autonomy means I have a say in my destiny, there were certain times in my life where I thought I was simply a passenger on someone else's life journey.

It first happened a few years out of college while I was working as a shop-floor supervisor at one of our factories. My job involved a three-shift operation in heat treating of steel parts—drawbars, gears, shafts, and large parts that went into transmissions and engines. I loved my job and the people I worked with. My routine was to show up a little after 6 a.m. and visit with the third shift operators, spend all day in the factory, and then visit with the second shift coming in at 4 p.m. and then head out around 5 or 6 p.m. I also came in on Sunday evenings to review production changes after weekend batch processing changes.

It was an incredible job for a 25-year-old kid. *I remember waking up in the parking lot at our factory at 6:00 a.m. not knowing how I got there.* Somehow, I had gotten up, showered, dressed, and driven to work, only to "wake-up" in the parking lot. My life had become such an embedded routine I barely sensed the moving pieces. My God what have I turned into????

The second time was later in my career after I accepted my first global position involving product marketing. This required travel to all regions of the world including Brazil, China, Germany, India, and Turkey, as well as all over the United States and Canada. It was an incredibly fast-paced job. At the same time, our third daughter was born. This meant we had to move from Dallas, Texas, to Augusta, Georgia, while adjusting from two kids ("man-to-man defense") to three kids ("zone defense"). Moving is always stressful, but this particular move was further complicated due to my almost immediate need to travel globally.

Early in this role, I remember going through Frankfurt-am-Main airport only to be notified that my four-year-old daughter had rolled out of bed at a hotel during the move and hit her head on the nightstand. This resulted in a trip to the emergency room to stitch up a small cut in her head. I remember thinking at that moment I shouldn't be in Germany—I should be there for my family, for my wife, and for my kids. My boss was great and even asked if I needed to head home, but I told them they would be fine. In the back of my mind, I struggled with not being there for them.

Later in this same role, I remember driving to work wondering how I was going to regain my life from an escalation that seemingly over-whelmed my work–life balance in one fell swoop. Most of the time I had no idea what time zone I was in; sleep came when and where possible, any rest was more or less always on the move.

I also struggled immensely for most of my career with taking prob-lems from work home with me. I recall vacations that were nearly ruined because of my inability to detach from the problems I faced at work. I distinctly remember asking myself during a 4th of July outing how I could possibly be taking time away from work given the problems I was facing. I lost sleep not only due to my immaturity at the time but also perhaps due to my vanity that the company could not go on without me. It was a brutal self-imposed hell that I guess I needed to experience. Maybe there is a certain point where being "too committed" is a bad thing where you can't let go and you need to feel the damage it does to learn the lesson.

Finding the right balance, or work–life "management" as some say, is an art. It will sneak up on you quietly like a thief in the night. *Literally*. It will rob you of your joy, happiness, sanity, and will drain the marrow out of your life if you are not careful.

Like quicksand, before you even know you are in trouble you have no way out. About the time you are conscious enough to sense what is going on, you also start to realize you need help. Acknowledging the need to lead a balanced lifestyle early, and developing robust habits before the consequences become dire, will serve you well in your career.

Leading Practices

Research and writing on work–life balance has grown tremendously in the past several years (Kelliher, Richardson, and Boiarintseva 2019). This is due in large part to the increasing pace of work and life. There are several best practices that can help guide us in the pursuit of Balance. They include:

- Balance versus Management
- Prioritization and Essentialism
- Presence
- Capacity
- Change

Balance Versus Management

Is the notion that work–life is a balancing act the wrong way to view the issue? Does it seem right that in order to be in "balance," you have to make a trade-off decision or offset various parts of your life against each other? Do you really check out of "life" when you are at "work" and vice versa?

Tony tried to live a more fluid, integrated life that allowed him to be 100 percent alive and well whether at home or work. He recognized that it was a continuous "cycle"—as opposed to believing that balance is a one-time "achievement" (Lupu and Castro 2021). In Confucian and Taoist traditions, this concept of personal harmony is called *wu-wei*.

Wu-Wei

Wu-wei is the art of embracing fluidity,
balance and flow in order to achieve action.

Below is an assessment from the Headington Institute (2022) for you to examine your own balance. Rate each statement considering the past month. The higher your total score, the better your well-being is likely to be. You can also identify some strategies to help you create that optimal balance by examining the items you rated lower.

---

0 | Almost Never   1 | Seldom   2 | Sometimes

3 | Often   4 | Almost Always

—— 1. I have at least one full day off work each week.
—— 2. I take some time for myself to be quiet,
　　　think, meditate, write and/or pray.
—— 3. I work no more than eight hours a day
　　　when not on deployment.
—— 4. I exercise for at least 25 minutes five days a week.
—— 5. I do something I find fun (e.g., play a game,
　　　go to a movie, read a book, etc.)
—— 6. I practice muscle relaxation, yoga, stretching,
　　　meditation, or slow-breathing.

—— 7. I share how I am feeling with at least
        one friend or my partner.

—— 8. I sleep well and get 7–8 hours of sleep a night.

—— 9. I am careful about what I eat and eat a balanced diet.

——10. I drink at least 2 liters of water a day.

——11. On balance I have more positive emo-
        tional experiences than negative.

——12. At the end of the day, I can leave the
        pressures of work behind.

——13. I slow down when I am becoming tired, run-
        down, and vulnerable to illness.

——14. There are people who care about me that I
        trust, to whom I can talk if I want.

——15. I do something I find creative or expressive.

——16. I feel I have the training and skills I need to do
        my job well.

——17. I stand up for myself, saying "no" when I need to.

——18. At work I take a brief break every two
        hours & switch tasks regularly.

——19. I spend time with trusted others who are part of a
        community of meaning and purpose (e.g., church group,
        community volunteers, work colleagues, book group).

——20. I feel good about my ability to communicate with others.

——21. I spend my time and energy doing what
        is important to me in life.

——22. I believe in my ability to accomplish goals,
        even when I encounter difficulties.

——23. I set realistic goals for my life and work towards them.

——24. I take good vacations.

——25. I can let go of mistakes I have made.

——26. I can manage conflict constructively.

——27. I can let go of grudges.

——28. I drink more than 1–2 alcoholic drinks,
        smoke, or use other recreational drugs.

Total Score: ——————

Prioritization

What good are core values in life? One of the best uses of core values is they can help you prioritize where you spend your most precious resource—your time. It's been said many ways by many people: we all have the same number of hours in the day. We need to work smarter, not harder. Stephen Covey would tell us "Put first things first" as part of his *7 Habits of Highly Successful People* fame (1997). David Allen in his book *Getting Things Done* would argue that we need to know why we are doing something so that we can effectively prioritize our time and actions (Allen 2015).

The bottom line is as our life evolves, so do our priorities. Early in our career, we may not have the demands of family upon us. We may not have the demands of supervision or escalating responsibilities at work. We may not be as involved in civic, religious, or social communities. But for most of us, the pattern of increasing demands of our time and energy as we grow in our lives means we are eventually placed in a position to have to make decisions and trade-offs about how best to spend our time. This requires knowing what is most important in our life and this eventually leads to prioritization.

Life is a series of trade-off decisions. One of our favorite tools to help leaders think about prioritization is an exercise called *Start | Stop | Continue*.

START

What activities would you like to start? They may improve processes, reduce waste, have a positive impact on your life, etc.

1. _____
2. _____
3. _____

STOP

What activities would you like to stop? They may be inefficient, waste time, or have a negative impact on your life, etc.

1. _____
2. _____
3. _____

CONTINUE

What activities would you like to continue? They may be activities you have tried successfully so they should become common practice.

1. _____

2. _____

3. _____

Presence

What does it mean to be 100 percent present wherever you are? Being so conscious of your present time and space that you can 100 percent focus on the people and events around you.

Clifford Nass, a brilliant psychology professor from Stanford University, has studied multitasking throughout his career (Ophir, Nass, and Wagner 2009). Tony attended a conference at Stanford in 2012 where Nass spoke about the relationship between technology and the social sciences and how people were managing this interface. His specific talk centered on "Can people really multitask"? His net conclusion—It's literally impossible to multitask and be effective at what you do.

There are always trade-offs. He said there might be a slight ability to multitask if one task is closely related to another—for example, when you are driving and a notification pops up on your dashboard display that there is a road closure ahead. In this instance, you may be able to drive and process the information quickly without any perceivable loss in performance of driving. However, if you were to be driving and an e-mail or text message pops up from your spouse telling you something important, and your mind shifts to process the e-mail, his research shows you would be compromised in your ability to safely drive the vehicle.

> *Act like wherever you are, that's the place to be.*
> —Mike Damone, Advice to Mark Ratner
> *Fast Times at Ridgemont High*

So, what's the most important lesson we can learn about being present? Be present. Wherever you are, that's where it's at. Period. Be where your feet are. If you are at work, do your best to be present for your employer and the people around you. When you are at home, do your best to be there for yourself and the people around you. This is made all the more difficult after the most recent pandemic that made working from home (WFH) a very common practice. However, done right, WFH can also contribute to managing balance.

Capacity

As we grow in our careers, we should be able to shoulder more problems in life. Think back 10 years and the problems you faced. Then think back five years, or maybe even one year. The problems you faced then should be easier to navigate today because of the experience we have gained by working through issues and resolving them. We should be a different person today than we were at some point previously in our life. That's the whole point about growth—we change. Hopefully, we become "more" and our changes result in "growth" even though the hard times may not always translate into the feeling of progress at the time. The following exercise helps compare the current and preferred balance among all your life's roles (Bloch and Richmond 1998).

BALANCING LIFE ROLES

Create a better life balance by examining your different life roles and making adjustments to the roles that are more important to you. Fill in the % of time you spend in each role and then the preferred % of time you would like. Take notice of the differences and adjust how you spend your time accordingly.

	CURRENT	PREFERRED
WORKER	◯ %	◯ %
LEARNER	◯ %	◯ %
SPIRITUAL PARTICIPANT	◯ %	◯ %
CITIZEN	◯ %	◯ %
FRIEND	◯ %	◯ %
AT LEISURE	◯ %	◯ %
SPOUSE	◯ %	◯ %
FAMILY MEMBER	◯ %	◯ %
	=100%	=100%

Changes Over Time

When solving complex equations in life, it all boils down to identifying the right parameters and then iterating and testing hypothesis after hypothesis until patterns turn into solutions. One massive variable that impacts us all is *time*.

How we change over time is important to recognize. We change. Our environment changes. Our priorities change. We hope it's all for the better and even when we fail, we learn and are better for it. It's OK to change how we deal with balance over time because our priorities change.

We should expect this and appreciate it as part of who we are.

As you think about balance, just realize that you are a work in progress and always will be. Your current situation is creating the ingredients for change to constantly evolve you in a positive direction. If you realize that your priorities will change over time you can begin to realize that your definition of balance will also evolve with them.

Essentialism

What are only those things that you can do, versus what others can and should do? A significant contribution to your ability to manage balance in your life is managing what you say "yes" to and what you say "no" to or delegate to others. If you take on too much, you are bound to struggle with getting done the most important, impactful things affecting your life. Taking on too much will result in suboptimizing your quality of life. The sooner you realize that you must focus on the highest and best good, the "essential" things, and let the other things wait or be done by others, the better your odds are of managing balance in your life.

> *Essentialism is a disciplined, systematic approach for determining where our highest point of contribution lies, then making execution of those things almost effortless.*
>
> —Greg McKeown, Author
> *Essentialism: The Disciplined Pursuit of Less*

Shared Wisdom: Lessons From the Road

When our community of leaders were asked about their careers, balance was one of the top themes to emerge from their collective recommendations. Attitude, ownership, comparing yourself to others, and feelings of inferiority or being an imposter all loomed large as they evaluated their careers.

Tony reflects below after 14 years into his career about how to balance seeking success against other important aspects of his life.

> *It all gets down to what you are willing to settle for. What do you define as success? What is good enough? There will always be an element of continuous improvement in life, but there has to be some sort of leveling process that measures the balance of all important things.*
> —Tony Thelen, Author
> Personal Journal, February 17, 2002 (34 years old)

A retired senior executive who also cofounded the Confidence Academy, a leadership development firm that focuses on female leadership, shares the challenges of managing a dual career against family and job demands.

> *Balancing a career and my family life was challenging. My husband also had a big career so there were many challenging times managing our home life. We had to learn to prioritize, be extremely organized, work together as a team, and let some things go. The key is to keep communicating and keep your family a priority.*
> —Kim Beardsley, Cofounder of Confidence Academy
> The Confidence Academy, Iowa, USA

A real estate executive who has owned his own firm for over 20 years shares how his commitment to his work led him to crisis and nearly a failed marriage, and how he recovered through seeking balance.

> *Working too hard almost cost me my marriage. Crisis woke me up. Reprioritized my life. Rebalanced. It worked.*
> —President and Founder
> Real estate industry, Iowa, USA

Catherine, a partner in her law firm, shares the impact of not finding the balance in your career early and offers encouragement that while still a challenge there are ways to accomplish it.

Yes, I would have done a better job at balancing personal/work time. As a young lawyer, for years, I spent too much time at work, on work. I practiced this way no matter what law firm I was in. This affected my marriage, my childrearing, stress levels and overall fulfillment. Today's workplace is still demanding but it is possible to better manage this.

—Catherine Wang, Partner
Morgan, Lewis, and Bockius, LLP, Washington DC, USA

Don, a retired marketing executive, shares advice he received early in his career about the regret that can come from sacrificing time with the family against a successful career.

A longtime Territory Manager was mentoring me for the position. He cautioned that he was nearing the end of his career and felt he had sacrificed his family in pursuit of his career which he loved but was somewhat disappointed with at the time. He warned that proper balance was needed for success.

—Don Worner, Marketing Manager (Retired)
John Deere, Tennessee, USA

Paul, a president and founder of a leadership consulting firm, shares how important conversations are in guiding the quality of our lives.

The quality of our lives will depend upon the quality of our conversations.
—Paul Axtell, President
Contextual Program Designs, Minnesota, USA

Many leaders reflected upon the sustaining value of relationships and family after a long career. Upon reflection, most leaders would not choose to work more if given the chance; rather they would choose to "work for their eulogy as opposed to the bottom line." They would invest in building sustaining relationships rather than the impermanent returns of tasks and projects.

Jim, a retired executive, shares the challenge of prioritizing opportunities to contribute to your career versus spending time with his family. Notably, he shares that as a leader the way he deals with this issue will impact others in his organization.

> *I would have had a better focus on work–life balance. As I look back at my career, I realized that many of the work activities I focused on weren't as important as the family activities that I missed out on. I realized that there will always be business issues to address, but that you will never again have the opportunity to watch your kids play that soccer game, dance, sing in school activities, etc. As a leader, if you prioritize your family, your employees will also feel empowered to do so.*
>
> —Jim Israel, President (Retired)
> John Deere Financial, Iowa, USA

Kathy, a retired executive, shares the wisdom she earned in dealing with challenges of work–life balance that were ultimately resolved by her owning the situation and setting boundaries.

> *The biggest problem I faced in my career was balance between my work life and my personal life. Business travel, long days and working weekends were not unusual and high expectations on my part made it hard for me to flip the switch between work and home. I finally reached a point where I realized I was the one that needed to set boundaries and carve out time for personal activities and not feel guilty about it. I needed to realize and accept that sometimes "done" was better than "perfect" and know in what situations this guideline made sense.*
>
> —Kathy Kearney, Vice President (Retired)
> John Deere Financial, Wisconsin, USA

Vaden, an executive in the learning and development field, shares succinctly the advice to work for your eulogy not just the bottom line.

You'll always need to balance both doing work and being a good human. You need to live and work for your eulogy not your institution's bottom line.
        —Vaden Spurlock, Director Field Learning and Development
                                                    Gap Inc., Illinois, USA

Managing all commitments to achieve balance doesn't happen without making very practical decisions. These leaders offer some simple—yet transformational—tips and tricks they used to realize balance in their lives. The last two reflections deal specifically with choosing supportive partners to navigate work and life together—this intimate personal advice is critically important to achieving professional success and maintaining balance.

Gary, a retired CIO executive, shares the practical advice of buying yourself "work–life" tickets.

I would create more work–life balance "tickets." I'd read somewhere that if you have a ticket to a sporting event, theater event, etc. that you always find a way to leave work on time to get there. I wish that I would have done that more often to this point.
        —Gary Scholten, Chief Information Technology Officer
                                                    (Retired)
                            Principal Financial Group, Iowa, USA

Jenny, a retired executive, shares the challenges of being a senior leader of a Fortune 100 company.

This is a bit of a cop-out, but my big, overarching challenge was the extremely high demands made on leaders of Fortune 100 companies. I was either working or thinking about work almost all of the time. I decided around eight years before my early retirement at age 46 that I'd save like crazy and get out ASAP.
        —Jenny Kimball, Retired Executive
                                        South Carolina, USA

Crystal, a software engineering leader, shares the personal advice she received many years ago about the importance of having a supportive partner at home and the tremendous influence this had on her career.

The best career advice I heard was at a Women in Engineering discussion. The question I had heard asked many times before was "how do you manage work–life balance and a demanding career?" I remember the answer particularly because of the way she started. The woman (who was a high level manager) said, "I know this is going to sound like personal advice, but I promise you, it's professional." She went on to say, "You need to really be careful about who you marry. If you plan on having a family, your spouse is the person that you will need to work out everything with. They are the person you are depending on if you are working late, or traveling. They are the person you are negotiating with when the kids have doctor appointments, get sick, or need someone at their soccer games. It's key to having balance in work and life, and being able to devote as much as you would like to your career." This advice has led many of the conversations I've had with my husband regarding my career. How much time works for me to dedicate to my family and also to my job? What kind of travel will work for my family? Here is where I aspire to go—are you willing to make the sacrifices that will require for me to do that (such as be the lead parent)? It's not exactly typical advice when you think of career advice, but for me, it has made a tremendous difference in ensuring I have a partner who supports where my potential could lead me.
—Crystal Wells, Software Development Manager
John Deere, Iowa, USA

A dean of a major college shared similar advice to Crystal's in how she dealt with work–life issues, noting the importance of managing sacrifices to make it all work out in the end.

The most important lesson I've learned is how to balance family and career. I have five children. The early years of my career allowed me to live a relatively balanced life. Work flexibility allowed me to meet the family demands, in partnership with my husband, while also meeting work demands. But managerial roles would change that. Because my husband had no such aspirations, the resolution was that my husband would quit work and stay at home with the kids. As I counsel

other women, I acknowledge that there isn't one answer to family /
work–life balance. In the end, someone will sacrifice in some way,
although maybe not everyone at the same time. Kids may sacrifice
because a parent cannot be engaged in an activity. A mother or father
may sacrifice a promotion to make sure he or she can engage with those
activities. The family may live on less income because only one person
works and a range of sacrifices take place. You can have it all but you
probably can't have it all at the same time.

—Business School Dean
Higher education, USA

In all these reflections, moderation is a key goal and way of life. In
order to realize balance, balance has to be a daily resolution.

Reflections: What's Your Story?

1. What are your main insights/takeaways from the chapter at this moment?

_____

_____

_____

_____

_____

_____

_____

_____

2. What are one to three goals/intentions you would like to set for yourself?

_____

_____

_____

_____

_____

_____

_____

_____

_____

Going Further: Questions, Readings, and References

Discussion Questions

3.1   Tony talked about how out of balance he was early in his career by waking up in the parking lot not knowing how he got there one day. What would you have done in his situation?

3.2   Many of our leaders talk about the challenges of a progressively more difficult career and holding it together in your personal life. How important is it to you to have balance in your life and what are you willing to do to preserve it?

3.3   How can focusing on being more present wherever you are at any moment in time improve your life?

3.4   What does wu-wei mean to you and how can you use it to help maintain balance in your life?

3.5   Since the COVID-19 pandemic, there have been many changes to professional life. What changes can you make to your life right now to create a better life?

3.6   What are the "essential" things in your life that you cannot do without, and what things do you deal with today that can be let go of?

Suggested Reading

Friedman, S., E.G. Saunders, P. Bregman, and D. Wademan. 2019. *HBR Guide to Work-Life Balance.* Boston, MA: Harvard Business School Review Press.

Kelly, M. 2011. *Off Balance: Getting Beyond the Work-Life Balance Myth to Personal and Professional Satisfaction.* New York, NY: Penguin Random House.

Knapp, J., and J. Zeratsky. 2018. *Make Time: How to Focus on What Matters Every Day.* New York, NY: Currency.

References

Allen, D. 2015. *Getting Things Done: The Art of Stress-Free Productivity.* New York, NY: Penguin Books.

Bloch, D., and L. Richmond. 2015. *SoulWork: Finding the Work You Love, Loving the Work You Have.* Abingdon, UK: Routledge.

Brass Tacks and Lilacs. 2022. *Balancing Life Roles.*

Covey, S.R. 1997. *The 7 Habits of Highly Effective Families*. New York, NY: St. Martin's Press.

Headington Institute. 2022. *Self Care and Lifestyle Balance Inventory*.

Kelliher, C., J. Richardson, and G. Boiarintseva. April 2019. "All of Work? All of Life? Reconceptualising Work-Life Balance for the 21st Century." *Human Resource Management Journal* 29, no. 2, pp. 97–112.

Lupu, I., and M.R. Castro. 2021. "Work-Life Balance Is a Cycle, Not an Achievement." *Harvard Business Review*. https://hbr.org/2021/01/work-life-balance-is-a-cycle-not-an-achievement

Ophir, E., C. Nass, and A.D. Wagner. 2009. "Cognitive Control in Media Multitaskers." *Proceedings of the National Academy of Sciences* 106, no. 37, pp. 15583–15587.

CHAPTER 4

Well-Being

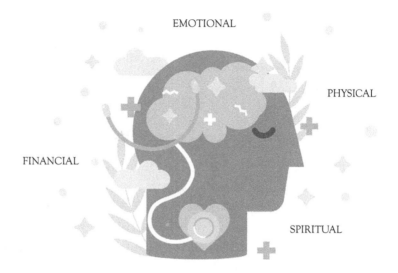

EMOTIONAL

PHYSICAL

FINANCIAL

SPIRITUAL

WELL-BEING

You have only one mind and one body for the rest of your life," Buffett says. "If you aren't taking care of them when you're young, it's like leaving a car out in hailstorms and letting rust eat away at it. If you don't take care of your mind and body now, by the time you're 40 or 50, you'll be like a car that can't go anywhere.

—Warren Buffet, CEO
Berkshire Hathaway, Nebraska, USA

Introduction

Sometimes having a clear goal and proper inspiration and motivation just aren't enough to get us where we need to be. Sometimes we don't have the right physical energy to be up to the task, or our endurance is low due to not taking care of our bodies. Sometimes we mentally wear down over time and have nothing left to take on the issues of the day. We have nothing left to help ourselves, let alone help anyone around us.

No amount of pep talk will make a difference if you have not the physical or emotional strength and energy to keep you performing at your best.

This chapter touches on the value of physical, mental, emotional, and spiritual well-being to make sure you have what you need to perform at your best. Making sure your "well-ness" tank is full will make sure you have the energy, vitality, and strength to bring out your "A" game.

Tony's Lessons From Personal Experience

As a kid, I really admired my older siblings. Ed, my oldest brother, went on to study biology at Iowa State University. In our house, we had a stairway that had a landing spot halfway up where it changed directions. In this landing spot was a bookshelf where Ed kept all his college books. I remember spending what seemed like days with Ed halfway up the stairs reading through his college books about birds, mammals, chemistry, biology, and all things in the natural world. These conversations carried me away to a new world that I couldn't wait to explore.

But there was another reason we stopped at the bookshelf to have these conversations. Ed couldn't walk up the entire staircase without resting to take a breath due to his severe asthma.

Ed went on to work for 34 years for the Iowa Department of Natural Resources and did every physical job asked of him despite dealing with chronic obstructive pulmonary disease (COPD). He was technically offered a disability program due to his doctor's assessment of his health, but he never seriously considered it. Being inactive and not contributing just wasn't in his nature. He also had understanding supervisors who helped him throughout his health ordeals. He retired several years ago and now spends his time hunting arrowheads, metal detecting, fishing, and bird watching. He tells me he is busier today than he was in the 9 to 5 world! I was proud of him when he was in college, during this career, and am now proud of him in his retirement. I remain one of his ardent admirers of how he took what was given to him and made the most of his opportunities.

Another person I admire is my wife Sheila for what she has taught me about health. In the early 2000s, Sheila and I were leading busy lives. My job took me across Texas and New Mexico nearly every week, we had just had our second child, and we had recently moved to Dallas where we did not have any local built-in support to help us with the transition. The wear and tear of daily life was taking a toll on us. We started to feel it in our health—I was gaining weight, we were both feeling lethargic after long days, and someone always seemed to be feeling ill or fatigued. It felt like we were losing control.

Sheila took the reins and decided we needed to learn more about natural health and how we could build our bodies better to improve our immune systems. Long story short, we removed sugar from our diets, cut out all the processed and packaged foods that we could, doubled down on organic food, drank enough water each day, and started consistent exercise in our weekly routine. The result? We haven't been to a doctor for illness in 15 years and we continue to learn more and more about how to invest in our health now so that we don't pay for it later.

As your career evolves, a keystone to your success will be how you approach wellness—both physical and nonphysical wellness. Achieving your goals in life will depend on whether you have the energy to get the job done. It's a prerequisite to leading a good career and a more fulfilling life.

You may be given challenges as my brother Ed was or you may be in perfect health. It's what you do with your situation and how you care for your well-being that counts. It always has and it always will. Becoming a billionaire will be little consolation if you lose your health in the process. The sooner you establish this as a key criterion of your success, the better off you will be.

Leading Practices

When it comes to wellness, there are many fads that come into fashion then disappear after a year or two. We also know that individual bodies respond differently to exercise, diets, and so on, and these responses can change over time. There are many aspects of wellness that are rooted in science and generally accepted. We can build a personal wellness practice built upon these proven techniques. The leading practices listed below represent a holistic approach to personal well-being:

- Regular Self-Assessment
- Wellness Wheel (Eight dimensions)
- Sleep
- Vision Board

Regular Self-Assessment

First, it is critically important to stay in tune with your own personal operating system. Just like when the "*Check Engine*" light flashes when your car needs service, your mind and body also give you signs about your well-being. The key is: *We must be paying attention!* Staying in tune with your mind/body over time is critical. In addition to regular physical and mental checkups with trusted medical professionals, one of the most highly recommended leading practices is to consistently monitor your own wellness using a holistic assessment like the Wellness Wheel as shown below (Yale School of Medicine 2019). Regularly checking-in on yourself produces at least two positive outcomes:

- First, it gets you into the practice of self-awareness. Assessing yourself in each dimension of wellness can serve as an early warning system especially when one dimension of wellness is slipping. We recommend regularly scoring yourself on a scale of 1 to 10 where 10 is "*Exceeding All Expectations*" and 1 represents a "*Dumpster Fire Rolling Downhill Backwards.*"
- Second, it improves your self-assessment accuracy. Imagine you were asked to estimate the number of jelly-beans in a jar. The first time you do it, it is very difficult and your guess likely wouldn't be very accurate. With repeated guesses, feedback, and experimentation, your accuracy will improve. Similarly, if you regularly assess your own well-being, you'll

Financial Wellness
The ability to identify your relationship with money and skills in managing resources. An intricate balance of the mental, spiritual, and physical aspects of money.

Spiritual Wellness
The ability to establish peace and harmony in our lives.

Physical Wellness
The ability to maintain a healthy quality of life without undue fatigue or physical stress.

Social Wellness
The ability to relate to and connect with other people in our world.

Intellectual Wellness
The ability to open our minds to new ideas and experiences that can be applied to personal decisions, group interaction and community betterment.

Emotional Wellness
The ability to understand ourselves and cope with the challenges life can bring.

Occupational Wellness
The ability to get personal fulfillment from our jobs or chosen career fields while still maintaining balance in our lives.

Environmental Wellness
The ability to recognize our own responsibility for the quality of the environment that surrounds us.

WELLNESS WHEEL

EMOTIONAL

INTELLECTUAL

OCCUPATIONAL

SOCIAL

ENVIRONMENTAL

PHYSICAL

FINANCIAL

SPIRITUAL

get very good at detecting any upward or downward devia-
tions. You'll get to know yourself even better and you'll be able
to recognize not only the most important ingredients for wellness (e.g., sleep, exercise, diet, connection, etc.) but also your
triggers (e.g., stress, pet-peeves, difficult times of year, etc.).

Wellness Wheel

Many of the topics in this book align to the eight dimensions of the
Wellness Wheel. For example, *Learning* (Chapter 8) supports your
intellectual wellness; *Purpose* (Chapter 5), *Balance* (Chapter 3), and
Relationships (Chapter 12) all support positive emotional wellness. Finally,
this entire book is designed to help support your occupational wellness!
The general introductions to these dimensions are provided below to
support your regular well-being assessment.

- *Intellectual wellness* is defined as "The ability to open our
  minds to new ideas and experiences that can be applied to
  personal decisions, group interaction and community betterment." Activities that improve intellectual wellness could
  include learning a new skill or language, taking on a new
  assignment, volunteering to serve a nonprofit organization.
- *Emotional wellness* is "the ability to understand ourselves
  and cope with the challenges life can bring." This is related
  to the emotional intelligence (EQ) which is the extent to
  which one is aware of and able to control emotions. EQ is
  not only important for wellness but also a cornerstone of
  leadership success (Goleman 2005). Activities that improve
  emotional wellness or EQ include monitoring your own
  emotional state/reactions, asking for feedback from a range
  of people in your life (e.g., a 360 assessment), remaining
  curious, and asking nonjudgmental questions in order to
  understand the why/motivations for your own behaviors
  and those of others. We all face adversity in life. One part of
  emotional wellness is cultivating *Resilience* (Chapter 15) to
  be able to cope with these stressful moments. Make sure you

make time for yourself, disconnect from the digital world on occasion, find sustainable methods for coping with stress, and seek professional help when it is needed. Remember, you are a priority!

- *Occupational wellness* is defined as "the ability to get personal fulfillment from our jobs or chosen career fields while still maintaining balance in our lives." In many ways this book is about developing the skill sets needed to achieve occupational wellness. Each chapter and the reflection questions are designed to help you attain a successful career and a more fulfilling life.

- *Environmental wellness* is a relatively new addition to the Wellness Wheel and is defined as "The ability to recognize our own responsibility for the quality of the environment that surrounds us." Activities that cultivate greater environmental wellness include any activity that deepens our connection with the natural world. Subsequently, this connection engenders a greater sense of stewardship and responsibility. Furthermore, care for our environment can involve local or global actions including everything from tending a garden to supporting large-scale environmental projects.

- *Financial wellness* is "the ability to identify your relationship with money and skills in managing resources. An intricate balance between the mental, spiritual, and physical aspects of money." We cover *financial literacy* extensively in Chapter 18, which is a fantastic starting place on the road to financial wellness. So many individuals are stressed due to financial resources and starting good practices early is crucial for the long term.

- *Spiritual wellness* is very simply defined as "the ability to establish peace and harmony in our lives." This could be membership in an organized religion, time in nature, meditation and yoga practices, or a feeling of belonging in a community. Regardless of the path or portfolio of activities you choose, find meaning, make time for things you enjoy, and focus on the positive aspects of your life.

- *Physical wellness* is "the ability to maintain a healthy quality of life without undue fatigue or physical stress." Sitting is the new smoking! Many have come to recognize that we are not designed to sit all day, every day; so if your career does not involve physical activity, what are other options for incorporating movement into your day? Is there a sport you want to try? Are you eating nutritious food most of the time? Are you getting sufficient sleep most days?

- *Social wellness* is "the ability to relate to and connect with other people in our world." No matter your personality style (e.g., introvert versus extravert), it is generally accepted that we are hard-wired for social connection. Our individual psychology is inextricably linked to our ability to relate and connect with others. As we've witnessed in the recent pandemic, this can take a variety of different forms including face-to-face interaction, virtual connection, social networks, gaming, or virtual/augmented reality collaboration! The good news is there are so many opportunities to connect, but the bad news is that we generally feel more disconnected that at any point in human history. As a result, social wellness is more important now than ever before! (Please see *Relationships* (Chapter 12) for more tips about developing your own social wellness.)

Sleep Is an Essential Ingredient, Not a Luxury!

In the last decade, there has been an explosion of research, findings, and public awareness extolling all the benefits of sleep. Poor sleep has been successfully linked to scores of nasty health outcomes such as increased body inflammation, heart disease, cancer, high blood pressure, stroke, dementia, and many others (Chirinos et al. 2019; Brody 2021).

In our own practice, we regularly see students who cram for finals by staying up all night only to realize several days later they can't think straight, and they've worked themselves into illness by depriving the body of sleep. Furthermore, we worked with countless executives who believe sleep is a luxury that reduces productivity. We worked with one CEO who was never quite able to shake a persistent cough for the first six months on the job, yet ironically, he prided himself on how little sleep he required to function! It wasn't until many months later he realized the correlation was indeed causation: his lack of sleep was contributing to his persistent infection (and was also affecting his cognitive performance and decision making)!

In the popular press, Elon Musk and Arianna Huffington had a very public spat about sleep and productivity, but it is Jeff Bezos who is probably the most famous executive advocate for sleep. He believes he owes it to his shareholders to get eight hours of sleep per night, because he privileges quality over quantity (Medium 2016).

> *Mostly, as any of us go through our lives, we don't need to maximize the number of decisions we make per day. Making a small number of key decisions well is more important than making a large number of decisions. If you shortchange your sleep, you might get a couple of extra "productive" hours, but that productivity might be an illusion. When you're talking about decisions and interactions, quality is usually more important than quantity.*
>
> —Jeff Bezos, CEO
> Amazon, Washington, DC, USA

There are so many useful tools to improve your sleep and sleep quality including your evening routine, sleep trackers, sleep aids, and more. For instance, we've used sleep trackers to demonstrate how stress, exercise, diet, weather, geography, or even the cycle of the moon can increase/decrease sleep quality by up to 15 percent! To start your sleep journey, you can access any number of good resources, but we recommend evaluating your sleep habits using a trusted diagnostic tool or tracking your sleep using a quality sleep tracker.

- WebMD Sleep Habits Assessment
- Sleep Cycle—Sleep tracker app

Vision Board

A vision board is simply a collage of pictures that help you live the life you want. It's a visual reminder of what is important in your life. Ideally it's something that you place in a prominent place to remind you daily of what your vision is for your life. It can be about your holistic life but in this chapter it can be particularly useful to reinforce aspects of wellness. Page through a few magazines, print off a few pictures from the Internet, and piece together the ideal version of yourself today.

Shared Wisdom: Lessons From the Road

A business financial analyst shares challenges faced after losing a job during the early days of the COVID pandemic.

> *I have been gainfully employed for over 30 years in my professional career. It was not until just recently that I was laid off due to a shift in the company's direction. This timing was just before the worst pandemic that the world has seen, at least in the last 100 years.*
>
> *As to be expected from any form of loss (refer to the Kubler Ross grief curve), I went through many emotions. I was able to work through the range of emotions and obtain further clarity. I am spending the time investing in myself. These areas include spiritual, physical exercise, self-reflection, and continued learning.*
>
> —Business Process Analyst
> Financial services, Illinois, USA

Sanjeev, an IT executive, shares the best advice he received related to wellness.

> *Best advice—Take care of your mind, body, and spirit.*
> —Sanjeev Satturu, VP, Information Technology
> Casey's General Stores, Iowa, USA

While reflecting on things he would change in his life, Paul explains not only the difficulty in showing up as a leader of a business and family, but also the important role of physical and mental wellness in his life.

> *That's a hard question, because it's sometimes difficult to see those decision points when you are in the middle of the scrum so to speak. But I would have to say if there is one regret, it's possibly that I didn't do*

more to take care of myself physically and mentally. It's important to keep your batteries charged. Important to your work, your longevity, your relationships, your happiness. I have always been willing to look at myself as the rock on which the water breaks—I think that's what a good leader does. Good leaders work harder than everyone else.

You lead by example, not by authority. Good leaders own the failures but deflect praise to others when good things happen as a result of hard effort. As a leader, as a driver of a business, even in my role as a husband, then my role as a father, my mentality was always to put my head down and push through for the greater good. At times it was exhausting for long periods of time. While in many respects it worked well for my business and my family, you can look back on that imbalance with some regret.

—Paul Schlueter, President
Flynn Wright, Iowa, USA

Kirk, a realtor, shares the challenges he faced throughout his career to make the right choices as his career and family both grew.

During my career I have been fortunate to hold positions as City Administrator, Developer/Contractor, Mayor, VP Banking, Restaurateur, Director of Marketing, University VP of Enrollment, President and CEO, Father etc. What I didn't understand about my career is how wrong leaders can be when they put on the leadership cape that says, "I got this." Do you really have it? How is your stress? How is your health? Do you monitor your whole health which I call SPEN Health (spiritual, physical, emotional, nutritional)? I never missed a kids' event, and it took beating cancer in 2010, and then not until 2017 did I realize that I should slow down, which happened to be just prior to my kids graduating college. I enjoyed seeing them as they had time. I dove deeper into leadership development and the power of a focused life. I asked myself several questions: How do I finish well? How do I leave a legacy? Am I in my lane or the lane I feel society expects me to be in? Who gets to write the story of my life? To whom do I give authority?

—Kirk Bjorland, Realtor
Coldwell Bankers, Iowa, USA

Todd, a founder and CEO of a data analytics firm, shares how it took years for him to adjust to improper balance and the importance of protecting your personal time.

> *I was working in a senior role and that required me to be on call outside of business hours, which led to a work–life imbalance. It took years to realize the effect of the imbalance on personal relationships, physical and mental health. Resolution was through a more balanced approach to life and protecting time allocated for those different facets to ensure physical and emotional restoration and opportunity for different growth experiences.*

—Todd Collinson, Founder/CEO
Oxford Informatics, Brighton, United Kingdom

Reflections: What's Your Story?

1. What are your main insights/takeaways from the chapter at this moment?

_____

_____

_____

_____

_____

_____

_____

_____

2. What are one to three goals/intentions you would like to set for yourself?

_____

_____

_____

_____

_____

_____

_____

_____

_____

Going Further: Questions, Readings, and References

Discussion Questions

4.1   How would you define and evaluate your wellness right now in your career? Remember to consider all aspects of health—physical, mental, emotional, spiritual, and so on. You may be doing better in one area than in another. Where are you strong? Where are you weak?

4.2   Many leaders share stories of how their wellness changed as they took on more responsibilities in their life and became more successful—what can you do today to get ahead of this and make sure wellness stays a priority in your life?

4.3   What parts of the Wellness Wheel are most concerning to you today? What can you do tomorrow to change this?

4.4   How much sleep do you get on a regular basis? What can you do today to sleep better?

4.5   What would be on your vision board today to help you lead a life of wellness? Make one today and put it in a prominent place to remind you of your ultimate potential.

4.6   Think about the most successful people you know today. How do they approach health and wellness?

Suggested Reading

Dalton-Smith, S. 2017. *Sacred Rest*. New York, NY: Hachette Books.

Kerr, R., J. Garvin, N. Heaton, and E. Boyle. 2006. "Emotional Intelligence and Leadership Effectiveness." *Leadership & Organization Development Journal* 27, no. 4, pp. 255–279.

Kross, E. 2021. *Chatter: The Voice in Our Head, Why It Matters, and How to Harness It*. New York, NY: Crown.

Leaf, C. 2021. *Cleaning Up Your Mental Mess: 5 Simple, Scientifically Proven Steps to Reduce Anxiety, Stress, and Toxic Thinking*. Grand Rapids, MI: Baker Books.

Web MD. 2021. www.webmd.com/sleep-disorders/sleep-habits-assessment

Tan, C-M. 2012. *Search Inside Yourself.* New York, NY: HarperOne.

References

Brody, J. 2021. www.nytimes.com/2021/12/06/well/mind/sleep-health.html?searchResultPosition=9

Chirinos , D.A., J.C. Ong, L.M. Garcini, D. Alvarado, and C. Fagundes. 2019. "Bereavement, self-reported sleep disturbances and inflammation: Results from Project HEART." *Psychosomatic medicine* 81, no. 1, p. 67.

Goleman, D. 2005. *Emotional Intelligence: Why It Can Matter More Than IQ.* New York, NY: Bantam Books.

Medium. 2016. https://medium.com/thrive-global/jeff-bezos-sleep-amazon-19c617c59daa

Yale School of Medicine. 2019. https://medicine.yale.edu/urology/education/residents/WW%20descriptions_341161_284_25240_v2.jpg

PART 2

Where Do I Want to Go?

Purpose, Goals, Clarity, and Feedback

CHAPTER 5

Purpose

| PURPOSE | LEGACY | TIME |
| | CRUCIBLE MOMENTS | PASSION |

If you don't know where you're going, any road will get you there.
—Lewis Carroll, Author
Alice's Adventures in Wonderland

Vision without execution is a daydream—but execution without vision is a nightmare.

—Japanese Proverb
Harvey Thompson
IBM

Introduction

A wonderful skill in life is to be able to "see the forest through the trees." It's important to be able to perceive the individual issues of our life but also have the perspective and context to understand the "big picture." Those who can see the big picture will be able to make better decisions and manage their journey well. Others will spend their life's fullest energy running into one tree at a time and will never see the forest through all the individual pain and agony.

Stopping to assess the big picture of your life is a critical step in building a strong foundation for a successful career and a fulfilling life. Laying out a vision is a daunting task but well worth the effort. It takes courage, faith, and humility. First, it takes courage to start and begin the process of getting your first draft on paper. Then comes the humble confidence to know that it isn't right, but with enough work and effort, you will master it. Finally, it takes a little faith to know that you are on the right path and the best is yet to come. This chapter gives you some food for thought as you take on the concept of shaping your life's vision.

Tony's Lessons From Personal Experience

In 2010 I had the benefit of hearing one of our board members speak in a small forum at Deere and Company headquarters. David Speer, CEO of Illinois Tool Works (ITW), was speaking about the role of a leader and how important it is to drive change. It was an awesome message and his biggest tool to create value at ITW were acquisitions and the 80/20 rule. ITW became experts at selecting companies to buy and transform into high-performing businesses. It was key to their growth, and as such, they built up a competency for successfully acquiring companies.

But what David told us really drove their performance was the 80/20 rule. Specifically, 80 percent of the results will come from 20 percent of the activity. He was a great speaker and like a lot of great speakers, he ended his talk with a personal challenge to each one of us. *David asked us to think about our purpose.* He asked us to do an 80/20 analysis on our life and challenged us to spend more time on the things that mattered the most.

He even took it one step further and asked us to take out our calendars and do a "calendar test"—that is, look back on the last 90 days and see if you spent your time on your highest priorities. He asked us, "Are you spending time focused on only the things you can do?" "Are you spending time on the most important things?" "Are you spending quality time with your family and loved ones?"

David spoke with deep conviction. We didn't know it at the time, but he was suffering from terminal cancer at the time. Sadly, he passed away less than a year later. I will always remember the way he asked us to think about our purpose and how he genuinely wanted us to live good lives. I'm also grateful to my company to put leaders like David Speer in front of us so we can learn from his experience.

Later, in 2011, I attended a seminar in Chicago called "Journey to the Extraordinaire" led by Alan Zimmerman. Both Sheila, my wife, and I attended, and we started to seriously think about the role of purpose in our lives. We had just moved nine times over 14 years to all parts of the United States, had three children, and I completed an MBA program. I was ripe for self-reflection and assessing what my true purpose in life was. I remember thinking I was living the life described by the following Bible verse:

All mortals are but a breath,
Mere phantoms, we go our way,
Mere vapor, our restless pursuits,
We heap up stores without knowing for whom.

—Psalm 39:7
Hebrew Bible

"Rowdy" Roddy Piper was a famous WWE (World Wrestling Entertainment, Inc.) Hall of Fame wrestler of WrestleMania legend. He used to taunt his opponents in many hilarious and entertaining ways. He famously claimed that "Just when they know the answer, I change the question!" Sometimes finding your purpose can feel like that. Just when you think you have arrived, somehow you find another part of the question that you didn't understand before. Maybe your life has changed, and you now hold new anxieties and stress that weren't there before.

At one point in my life, my purpose was to get a good education. It truly seemed like that was all that mattered and when that was accomplished things would fall into place. After that, it was replaced with getting a good job—and if I could only take care of that one goal, things would miraculously fall into place. Then I started asking myself if I was truly using my talents to the best of my abilities. Soon, it wasn't good enough just to have a job, but I wanted to align my ideal job with my specific skills to help me realize my full potential. Then I got married and it changed to "How could I be a good employee and a good husband?" A few years later a child arrived and then it grew to include "Being a good employee, husband, and father?"

Today, I think a lot about giving back to others as so many have given to me. After my experience with David Speer and Alan Zimmerman, I began to write down my purpose and set a few annual goals that I keep in a binder. My purpose is always the first page, and it gets looked at a few times every year. The first question is "Am I living my life on Purpose," and the second is "What about my purpose should change given what's going on in my life?" The process works for me and I believe I've been more intentional about how I spend my time.

Sometimes life can feel like you are plowing through life taking on more challenges and less like you are "settling down." My purpose was pretty clear earlier in my life—just take the next step and live life to its fullest and things will work out. When you get a job with more responsibilities, if you start a family, as you grow roots in a community, things tend to get more complex. My life was like a Christmas tree, and every year that came and went there were more ornaments to manage.

No matter where you come from or who/what you aspire to be, it can be tremendously beneficial to seek and define/refine your purpose throughout your life. Once you clarify your personal and/or professional purpose, a vision of the life you'd like to achieve and the legacy you will leave, you can then live your life in alignment with that clarity. Having a vision about how you want your life to work out is like having a best friend that you can always go to for a deep conversation. It can be one of the most important conversations of your life—I recommend you start today!

Leading Practices

People follow leaders who have a clear purpose and they also join companies that pursue a clear mission and vision. In fact, 9 out of 10 workers believe companies should have a purpose that extends to the benefit of all stakeholders.

Interest in individual and organizational purpose has taken off in recent years, especially since the COVID-19 pandemic has caused significant disruption, reflection, and introspection. There are several leading practices that can help get you started on thinking about your purpose and vision:

- Crucible Moments
- Purpose Model: Find. Live. Tell.
- Start With Why
- Time Tracking + Reflection

Life's Crucible Moments

Sometimes purpose is defined by the crucible moments in your life. For instance, when have you felt the most anxiety in your adult life (professionally or personally)? Or, when have you felt the most secure in your adult life?

By definition, these are experiences that transform your identity or your perspectives. Usually, in these crucible moments, we can see the fullness of our world with utmost clarity. Therefore, the answers to these questions about your life's crucible moments can help you focus to identify the core of what is most meaningful in your life. When you have answered these questions, you can more easily identify the commonalities and that should help clarify your purpose. Reflect on question 5.2 in the concluding section of this chapter to identify possible crucible moments in your own life.

Find. Live. Tell: Purpose Model

At Porter Novelli—a leading communications strategy consulting firm—they believe in the power of their model Find. Live. Tell. to help define a team or organizational purpose. A company cannot live with purpose without first finding and understanding its unique ambition. And a company certainly cannot "tell" its purpose to the world without first living it. In this time when decisions must be made in a blink of an eye that could impact hundreds of thousands of employees and millions in communities around the world, companies must have a North Star to guide them. That North Star, that Purpose, acts as a filter through which leaders and businesses can make the right decision, because an organization understands at an innate level where its values and priorities lie (Cole 2020).

Start With Why

In his book *Start with WHY*, Simon Sinek has created a very intuitive way to help us all discover, define, and live out our purpose (Sinek 2009). His "Golden Circle" framework invites us to answer the most basic of questions: Why? + How? + What? Furthermore, he explains how these core questions align to the core functioning of our brain.

SIMON SINEK'S "GOLDEN CIRCLE"
THE SCIENCE BEHIND WHY?

The purpose, cause or belief that drives you. Why you get up in the morning.

The unique talents that make you special.

The actions you take toward achieving your WHY.

WHY
HOW
WHAT

LIMBIC BRAIN
NEOCORTEX

The **Limbic Brain** is responsible for all feelings, behavior and decision making.

The **Neocortex** is responsible for rational and analytical thought and language.

Time Measurement/Management

We cannot manage what we do not measure. "Show me how you spend your time and I'll show you what you believe is most important," said K. Clothier. As Tony described earlier, the time-measurement calendar exercise can be very powerful to illustrate how you've defined your priorities or purpose. Practically, it is an easy exercise with a few key steps (Britton and Tesser 1991):

- Track how you spend your time over a couple of weeks or months.
- Sort your behavior by time spent on each activity or task.

- Then, rank each activity by priority and plot it on a graph (time spent versus priority).
- Identify lessons learned, and what needs to change, and create a schedule.
- Make a plan to change and remember that priorities can change over time.

Time Management Worksheet							
Time	Sunday	Monday	Tuesday	Wednesday	Thursday	Friday	Saturday
07:00							
08:00							
09:00							
10:00							
11:00							
12:00							
01:00							
02:00							
03:00							
04:00							
05:00							
06:00							
07:00							
08:00							
09:00							
10:00							
11:00							

Shared Wisdom: Lessons From the Road

The following comments contain reflections on purpose from our community of leaders. One common theme that emerges is about individuals' powerful realization they can define/shape/influence their own purpose. We also see the importance of making sure that you are aligning to your envisioned legacy as you move through your career.

Lisa, a system engineer, shares the challenges she faced during her journey toward finding her purpose that ultimately led to a successful career and a more fulfilling life.

I wasn't happy with the job I had, even though it was hard to get with an extremely successful company and was in the degree I worked hard to obtain—mechanical engineering. My roommate noticed I was always helping out with computer/internet support at my job and also that I enjoyed it and suggested I should quit my job that I hated and go into some type of software training, coding, etc. So I did. With a $20,000/year pay cut. Best decision I ever made—I was 27 years old and through teaching, training, consulting, contracting—you name it—I essentially was gaining skills and education on the job and am now, and have been for some time, a full-time programming engineer making a salary I am very comfortable with at a company I love.

—Lisa Warne, Systems Engineer
MyCropTechnologies, Minnesota, USA

Jasmine, a real estate agent, shares the power in finding her purpose and leaving behind someone else's story about her life.

My purpose. I was living someone else's purpose. I decided to change my environment and create my own purpose.

—Jasmina Salkic-Shutte, Broker Associate
EXIT Realty Capital City, Iowa, USA

Eugene, a CEO of an insurance company in South Africa, shares the limits of money, titles, and fame.

Life is about purpose and not just about money, title, and fame. To find your purpose search for what you are great at, then try to match this strength with something that you care about, enjoy, or are really interested in.

—Eugene Strauss, CEO
Insurance company, Johannesburg, South Africa

Amy, a former controller of a major Fortune 100 company who made a career change to a director of finance of a local nonprofit, shares the power in honoring the desire to have meaningful and purposeful work and aligning it with personal values.

The biggest problem I faced was the realization that the company I started to work for right out of college had evolved, and I no longer aligned with the values and strategy of the company. I desired meaningful and purposeful work, which I no longer felt with this company. I resolved this by leaving the company and working for a nonprofit organization with a mission I aligned with.

—Amy Yeager, Director of Finance
Nonprofit organization, Iowa, USA

Albert, a leader in architecture customer experience, and Russ, a founder and owner of a communications consulting firm, share the power of having a vision for your career and working on that vision to have the career you want.

Identify a vision for your career—a career objective. Make a plan to achieve it and execute it with discipline. I learned this lesson when I was 25 years old ... at the beginning of my career.

—Alberto Flores, Head of Architecture CX
Electrolux, North Carolina, USA

When working on your career plan, don't look at the jobs that are there today ... look at where the jobs will be tomorrow. That requires vision.

—Russ Walker, Principal Consultant and Senior Writer
WalRuss Communications, Consulting and Creative, Iowa, USA

Mark, an executive coach and Director of a leadership consulting business, shares a pivotal experience when he paused his career to reflect on who he was becoming. His inner exploration created a renewed vision and commitment that he continues to live to this day.

I was not fulfilled in my first career, and it was creating poor quality of life for me in my late 20s and early 30s. I put a hold on work and traveled to SE Asia at 34 years old. It was there that the quiet passion of my next career, coupling the experience of my first career, revealed itself. I ultimately went back to graduate school for an MA in I/O Psychology and simultaneously launched my career as a leadership development consultant and executive coach.

—Mark Cappellino, Senior Managing Director

Ankura, Tennessee, USA

Reflections: What's Your Story?

1. What are your main insights/takeaways from the chapter at this moment?

_____

_____

_____

_____

_____

_____

_____

_____

_____

_____

2. What are one to three goals/intentions you would like to set for yourself?

_____

_____

_____

_____

_____

_____

_____

_____

_____

_____

_____

Going Further: Questions, Readings, and References

Discussion Questions

5.1   Tony noted how his purpose evolved as his life changed. What is your purpose today? Write it down somewhere and revisit and update it every three to six months.

5.2   Leaders often talk about challenges they face or difficulties in their career that led them to a greater insight on their purpose in life. What challenges have you faced, or are facing now, that may be the key to unlocking your purpose or vision for your life?

5.3   The three following questions can be used to help you identify your purpose through triangulation. In fact, you can draw three overlapping circles in a Venn diagram and write your answers to each within the circles. Where they overlap may lead you to new insights about your purpose.

•   What are you good at? (*Where do your talents best take you?*)

•   What makes a difference? (*What can you make a living doing?*)

•   What do you love doing? (*What speaks to your passions?*)

5.4   Think of two leaders you know personally whom you admire in some way. Why do you admire these individuals? How might this inform your dreams and aspirations as you envision your own legacy? How can you do something tomorrow to emulate those what you admire about these leaders?

5.5   What are the five most important parts of your life today? What is the highest outcome that can be achieved in all five of them? Write your answers down and then ask yourself if anything needs to change to "make it happen."

Suggested Reading

Andrews, A. 2014. *The Seven Decisions: Understanding the Keys to Personal Success.* Nashville, TN: Thomas Nelson.

Burnett, B., and D. Evans. 2016. *Designing Your Life: How to Build a Well-Lived, Joyful Life*. New York, NY: Alfred A. Knopf.

Dalio, R. 2017. *Principles*. New York, NY: Simon and Schuster.

Hyatt, M., and D. Harkavy. 2016. *Living Forward: A Proven Plan to Stop Drifting and Get the Life You Want*. Grand Rapids: Baker Books.

Loehr, J. 2007. *The Power of Story*. New York, NY: Free Press.

Zimmerman, A. 2015. *The Payoff Principle*. Austin, TX. The Greenleaf Book Group Press.

References

Britton, B.K., and A. Tesser. 1991. "Effects of Time-Management Practices on College Grades." *Journal of Educational Psychology* 83, no. 3, pp. 405–410.

Cole, M-A. 2020, May. *Employers of the Future—We Can Do Better*. Talent Management Institute. www.tmi.org

Sinek, S. 2009. *Start with Why: How Great Leaders Inspire Everyone to Take Action*. Penguin.

CHAPTER 6

Goals

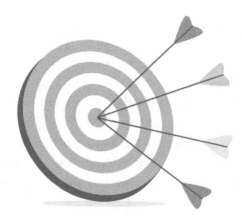

GOALS

SPECIFIC
MEASURABLE
AGGRESSIVE
ACHIEVABLE
REALISTIC
RELEVANT
TIME BOUND

What is the primary reason people fail to realize their goals? Answer: Fear.

Know what you want to accomplish, develop a plan for accomplishing it, commit to your goal, make the time to be successful and make the hard choices that propel you toward your goal.

Also, remain flexible as plans are sure to change.

—Tyler Hogrefe, Business Insights Manager
John Deere, Kansas, USA

Introduction

Most people understand the concept of goal setting and why it's important to have goals in life. They know that their odds of succeeding increase if they have written down their life goals. They know they will accomplish more, become more, and mean more to others in the world by being goal-driven. The odds of leading a successful career and a more fulfilling life increase by having written goals. Despite the power of goal setting very few people have taken the time to write down their life own goals.

This chapter aims to give you the tools and techniques to get good at understanding, setting, and accomplishing goals. If you make goal setting a habit, and embrace the process, and master it over your life, your odds increase dramatically of accomplishing more than you ever dreamed.

Tony's Lessons From Personal Experience

As early as perhaps ten years old, I remember thinking I just wanted to grow up to be a professional at something and contribute to a good brand. That, and star in basketball, baseball, and football, and get married, and have a family, and own a log home on the Yellowstone River. Oh, and I wanted to own a tiger. And yes, I wanted to buy a nice new home for my Mom and Dad whenever they got around to retiring. I have a list where I wrote all this stuff down when I was a kid. Even back then I was setting goals!

Or was I?

As I think back, I believe I was more a dreamer and less of a goal setter. Drifting off in math class in second grade dreaming about fishing in Montana and having the presence of mind to write it down on your Big Chief tablet doesn't quite qualify as goal setting.

When I got to college, I played a lot of basketball. I would say during my freshman year for every hour I studied there was an equal hour spent in the Field House gymnasium at the University of Iowa. That amounted to about two to four hours per day, and I was in the best shape of my life, playing the best basketball of my career. On good days, I was "picked up" to play on teams with Iowa basketball stars BJ Armstrong, Roy Marble, Ed Horton, and Quinn Early who was a star for the football team and later in the NFL (National Football League). I remember Roy the most because he always complimented me on my baseline defense and told me I was better on the pick and roll than most of the others.

A goal I had developed that year was to play for the "Gray Team"—a team of walk-ons who practiced with the team. For each Iowa home game one or two were chosen from the gray team to suit up for games, never getting in unless it was a blow-out. I shared this goal with a group of alumni from my hometown during a tailgate at a football game and they told me I was dreaming and could never do it. Even though I was routinely scrimmaging with the team, and I knew I had a good game, their influence on me was overwhelming. I never followed through in trying out for the Gray team.

To this day, it's one of my life's bigger regrets. First, because I think I would have had a pretty good shot at making the team. And second, it was an example of where *I let someone else's story about me be greater than my own.* Daniel Pink, in his book *The Power of Regrets,* would call this a "boldness" regret. It's been over 30 years and it still bothers me that I didn't give myself a shot at the team.

About five years into my career, I started writing down what I really wanted in life. When I started working for John Deere there was no such thing as performance management type systems that kept track of goals and performance reviews. Probably, the first serious conversation I had around goals took place in a two-day marriage encounter retreat I did with my wife when I was 25. We talked about what we wanted in life—family, finances, career, faith, and so on—we each have the spiral bound notebook from that process 30 years ago.

It was a good process—talk, write things down, retreat to a solitary space to think, get back together and talk some more, and over the course of the weekend you got to know each other a little better. The idea was the odds of you having a long-term relationship should improve.

We all have experience in goal setting even if it's just laying out an agenda for the day or if it's keeping track of a lifetime experience list. You may have thought a lot about goals or very little, but if you want to have a positive and constructive career, and you want the odds to be stacked in your favor, now is the time to start using this simple but powerful motivational technique.

Leading Practices

There is significant evidence linking good goal setting with performance improvement. Whether the goals are personal or professional, consider these elements when setting goals for yourself or designing them for your team members.

- Why Set Goals?
- SMART Goal Design
- Power of Data
- Accountability

Why Set Goals?

Each year for the last 10 years, Tony has spent his Christmas vacation doing two things: writing goals for the next year and reviewing the previous year's goals and writing letters to people who meant the most to him. It is a simple process he started after attending one of Alan Zimmerman's seminars on goal setting. It starts with evaluating his life's purpose, followed by goals that range from faith, financial, learning, work, family, and health. These binders are called his "Purpose, Goals, and Plans" books and they've served as the foundation of his personal and professional success.

Throughout the year, the binder morphs into a scrapbook of sorts. Everything that matters throughout the year goes into the binder—the tickets to the game with his daughters, the program for their high school and college graduation, a picture of roses he brought home to surprise his wife, pictures of a trip with a friend flyfishing, funeral cards, wedding invites, graduation invitations, cards and letters received from people, and so on. Everything goes into the binder if it is part of achieving a goal related to how Tony has defined success in his life. The last part is really important—thinking back on the year and saying "thank you" to people who have meant to the most to you.

SMART Goals

Make sure your goals are SMART (Doran 1981), which is an acronym meaning specific, measurable, aggressive (but also achievable), realistic (and relevant), and time-bound. In essence, they should not sound like the typical New Year's resolutions we hear. Compare, for instance, "I want to lose weight" with "I am going to lose ten pounds over the next two months." Or another common one, "I want to read more" versus "I am going to read twelve books this summer."

If possible, reflect on ways you might break up these SMART goals into quick wins or "thin slices" that build up to the larger objective you wish to meet. Small victories along the way will help keep you on track.

Write the goals down—which forces you to stop, think and clarify—and put them somewhere you will see them regularly. This also creates an artifact you can return to later for reflection and refinement.

Carefully prioritize the goals you've set for yourself if there are more than you can do at once. Acknowledge any dependencies or logical sequences, for example, do you want to learn Italian before you schedule that cooking vacation in Italy so you can get a little more out of time with locals during the trip?

Power of Data

One very simple framework we use for setting goals is called the OKR Framework—Objectives and Key Results. We've generally found that individual development plans should have no more than three high-level objectives. The key results should generally consist of metrics that illustrate progress toward the objectives. Finally, the initiatives are specific tasks or projects that align/support the chosen key results. By way of illustration, if you had an objective of wanting to learn more about computer science, your metric could be a chosen level of proficiency in a specific coding language, and your project would be successfully completing an online class in that language by a certain deadline. For a more complete explanation of OKR's please see the Doerr and Page's book *Measure What Matters* shown in the reference list at the end of this chapter.

Accountability

Decide if you need support staying on track. Are you intrinsically or extrinsically motivated? When relying on intrinsic motivation, be sure you are aligned with your passions and values, consider creating a vision board to have a reminder, and track progress to help you maintain focus on the experience (Williams 2020). If you thrive on extrinsic awards or recognition, consider finding a friend, coach, or mentor who is willing to hear about your progress from time to time and serve in that capacity to help you along the way.

Screen goals for areas where you have individual control and agency. For example, getting a promotion at work may depend on a variety of factors beyond your control. However, acquiring experiences and learning new skills so you're qualified for the promotion is within your power to manage.

Setting goals can have a profound impact on your career and where you end up in life. Make sure you use goal setting to your advantage keeping in mind the following: *Don't let someone else's story dominate how you think about your career.*

Shared Wisdom: Lessons From the Road

The following comments contain reflections on goal setting in the workplace from our community of leaders. You'll notice that they share some common lessons—start now, be clear, think ahead!

Tina, a head volleyball coach at the collegiate level, shares her journey of discovery in discerning the goals she had for her career, and how various experiences have shaped her professional life.

When I first started my career, I thought that Division I was the way to go. After working with two very different coaches at the Division I level, I quickly realized that it's the people you surround yourself with that matter and not the division in which you coach. My daughter was born while I was coaching in my first full-time D1 job and the head coach at that time turned out to be someone that was not the mentor I was hoping for. His tenure there ended and unfortunately so did mine. I definitely learned a LOT about how I did and didn't want the coaching profession to be for me and my future. From there I went to Iowa State and joined a staff that was knowledgeable and driven. I was out of my comfort zone at times but loved the challenge. I was lucky to develop a solid relationship with the ISU head coach and from there, her recommendation was a huge part of why I was offered the job at Grand View. From there I knew I was in the right place. I was surrounded by coaches who were also raising families and that's exactly what I wanted at the time. I wanted my family to be a priority. I look at some of my friends now and realize just how much they sacrificed for their careers, and I smile because of the choices I made.

—Tina Carter, Head Volleyball Coach
Grand View University, Iowa, USA

A director in the automotive industry shares the power of goals and the value of working on them early in a career.

Be more proactive with my career, think bigger than today, tomorrow, or next week. Have a 10-year goal and create a plan to accomplish it in one year. For a large part of my career, I deflected many key decisions to my leadership instead of being more front footed with my goals and desires. Additionally, I was so focused on the "now" that I didn't spend enough time telling my own story and defining my personal mission and vision. I have had a successful career, but I believe taking these actions earlier would have enabled me to reach much higher levels.

—Director
Automotive Industry, Michigan, USA

Jean, a business development executive, and former executive in supply management for a Fortune 100 company, shares the limits of working hard if you don't have an intentional plan for your career.

Working hard won't necessarily get you the career you desire. You need to create a general career path and let leadership know your interests in order to help open doors. I got this advice about 7 years into my career at Deere and it helped greatly!

—Jean Bowen, Energy Business Lead
River Valley Cooperative, Iowa, USA

Latitia, a digital product owner, shares how having an open and trusting conversation about her career led to a change in mindset, and new career opportunities.

The best advice I received in my career came from a Managing Director when I was at a mid-career stage, holding an IT Manager position. He and I were closely collaborating to deliver a critical project to the Business. One day, he invited me to his office for a chat. He wished to know more about my career aspirations, my willingness to grow professionally. At that time, I was not considering any particular career progression, after 12 years spent in the same position, I was enjoying a routine life at work. He finally advised me: "you should target to play a different role in 3 years' time at the latest and do your utmost to reach that goal." Subsequently, he helped me to revisit my development plan, found a coach for me and also became my mentor. This leader changed my mindset and triggered the fresh focus I gave to my career. I left behind my daily routine to focus on my new professional goal, dedicated a lot of time, energy, passion... and finally succeeded to get a new role 27 months later.

—Laetitia Baratelli, Digital Product Owner
John Deere, Luxembourg

Michael, a communications executive, shares advice to take control of your career early and the power of asking for help.

I would have started to "take control" of my career much earlier. Too often, early on, I allowed my managers to determine the direction and course of my career. I could have been more focused on where I wanted to be and asked for help getting there.

—Michael Gustafson, Deer's Landing
Owner, Illinois, USA

Mike, a retired marketing executive and chairman of an agriculture business council, shares the importance of being open minded about future opportunities and seeking help from coaching and mentoring on career development.

Best advice was to not limit my thinking to what I see around me today. Think about the future and where you would like to be short-term and long-term. The job I had at the time was one I assumed

I would have throughout my career. Up to this time, I had no real coaching from anyone about career development and other opportunities that might match my skill set.

—Mike Johanning, Former Chairman
Agriculture Business Council of Kansas City, Missouri, USA

Reflections: What's Your Story?

1. What are your main insights/takeaways from the chapter at this moment?

_____

_____

_____

_____

_____

_____

_____

_____

_____

2. What are one to three goals/intentions you would like to set for yourself?

_____

_____

_____

_____

_____

_____

_____

_____

_____

_____

Going Further: Questions, Readings, and References

Discussion Questions

6.1 Tony talked about listening to other people's versions of his life story and regretting how their narratives shaped his decisions at the time. Whose stories about your life are you listening to today? What can you do tomorrow to discard any negative influence?

6.2 Many leaders talk about the need to have a goal for their career and aim for both short-term and long-term objectives. Where are you today with your short-term and long-term goals? Write them down and revisit them often.

6.3 Matthew and Jeff talk about the importance of a SMART goal—specific, measurable, aggressive (stretch), realistic, and time-bound. Create a few SMART goals for your life today. How did this process change the way you create goals, and how did it influence your work in achieving them?

6.4 Find someone you trust to share your goals in life with. Make sure to have your goals written down before the conversation. How did you feel writing down your goals and sharing them with someone? Did the experience change the way you think about your goals?

6.5 Say thank you to people who help you. Whatever it is you do in your life, there are a mountain of people who have helped you along the way. Take the time to say thanks. It doesn't cost anything, but it is important?

Suggested Reading

Hyatt, M. 2018. *Your Best Year Ever: A 5-Step Plan for Achieving Your Most Important Goals*. Grand Rapids, MI: Baker Books.

McKeown, G. 2014. *Essentialism: The Disciplined Pursuit of Less*. New York, NY: Crown Business.

Pink, D. 2022. *The Power of Regret: How Looking Backward Moves Us Forward*. Riverhead Books.

Tracy, B. 2010. *Goals! How to Get Everything You Want—Faster Than You Ever Thought Possible*. San Francisco, CA: Berrett-Koehler Publishers.

References

Doerr, J., and L. Page. 2018. *Measure what Matters: How Google, Bono, and the Gates Foundation Rock the World With OKRs.* New York, NY: Portfolio.

Doran, G.T. 1981. "There's a SMART Way to Write Management's Goals and Objectives." *Management Review* 70, no. 11, pp. 35–36.

Williams, B. October 12, 2020.. "How to Leverage Intrinsic Motivation for Personal Fulfillment." *Forbes.* www.forbes.com/sites/theyec/2020/10/12/how-to-leverage-intrinsic-motivation-for-personal-fulfillment/?sh=752e8f3277a8

CHAPTER 7

Clarity

CLARITY
COMMUNICATION
INTEGRITY
HONESTY

If you can't explain it simply, you don't understand it well enough.

—Albert Einstein
Theoretical Physicist

Introduction

Sometimes life gets a little complex and hard to figure out. Sometimes life gets a lot complex. The days and weeks blend together and can get cloudy. We can lose our way if we aren't careful. Being conscious enough to perceive you are lost and slowing down enough to perceive what is going on is an important step. If you can do this, you have earned the right to stop, pause, and take on one of life's most important tasks.

Sometimes we need to simply assess the situation and get clear about what is going on.

Gaining clarity, and being clear about what you have going on, is something you will come to value over your lifetime. Being clear about your own intentions and being able to communicate clearly are important.

So is assessing a situation and getting clear about what is really going on. Being able to crystallize what is important among the noise in our life will pay you dividends every day of your life. It will help you focus on what is important and let the rest fall away like water off a duck's back.

Tony's Lessons From Personal Experience

Denny Mills was always excited about some venture in life. By day he worked for the IT department at John Deere, but when he wasn't working at Deere he was always involved in some venture of some sort. He was organizing basketball tournaments, running in marathons, or raising emus before raising emus was a thing. Flying experimental aircraft was one of my favorites. One time I saw what looked like a go-cart with a fan behind it under a huge parachute about 400 feet above Cedar Falls. Yep—it was Denny trying out a new aircraft he bought. Denny always seemed to have a lot going on and I never could figure out how he kept it all held together.

One time Denny decided to organize a celebration for a coworker who was retiring. He ordered three dozen large cookies from a local bakery in Waterloo. The person taking the order asked him to clarify to make sure he wanted the "large" cookies. Denny said he absolutely wanted the biggest cookies they made. About two weeks later, when Denny went to pick up the cookies, he discovered he had made a "huge" mistake. As it turns out, the bakery made a really large cookie that was 15 inches in diameter, and they had prepared 36 of them for Denny's party.

Turns out "large" to one person isn't the same "large" to another when it comes to ordering cookies!

It's one thing to have a misunderstanding with a local bakery, but what if a misunderstanding gets in the way of millions of dollars of scrap? Or you lose a key account? Or you are looked over for a key promotion? Or you lose your job? Or you hurt someone important in your life?

I remember one time when I was the manager of global marketing for small tractors in 2007 when a lack of clarity cost us a very expensive lesson. It was a newly created role and my job was to coordinate and align a global portfolio of tractors that were designed and built in eight locations around the world. Without global coordination, there was substantial overlap and inefficiencies to the point where my colleagues in India were flying to Brazil to sell their tractors to the Brazilian market while at the same time the team in Brazil was flying to India to sell their tractors to the Indian market. It wasn't anyone's fault—it's just the way the company grew up and now it needed to change in order to get us to the next level in our evolution.

One important project I inherited during this time was a design of a new tractor that would serve several global markets. In the later stages of development, prototypes of the tractor were built. At that point in the program, R&D dollars had been spent on design, tooling, and prototypes at our suppliers and in our own factories. When it came time to review the prototype with customers and dealers, it was immediately rejected with several specific concerns in the design. Customers and dealers were crystal clear in their feedback. A follow-up meeting was held to review what had gone wrong and it was discovered that assumptions were made early in the design process that were not valid and communications about the acceptance of the design by customers were vague. This outcome was a huge let down that wasted precious research funding and over a year in development time. With greater clarity, all of this could have been avoided and our product would have reached the customers and dealers much earlier than it eventually did. In the end, this experience was a great lesson for many people who went on to lead successful careers.

As life evolves, and our world becomes more complex, one of the biggest slippery slopes is thinking everyone thinks the way you do. Not only is this a career derailer but it can lead to problems in personal and professional relationships. You can leave a meeting thinking everyone is on the same page, only to learn after it's too late that half the room left with a completely different expectation. Everyone heard the same thing, but everyone walked away with a different understanding.

Unfortunately, it happens all the time and it is so easy to avoid. Sometimes it gets down to someone having the leadership presence to step up before adjourning and repeating what the expectations are and asking, "Are we clear?" In some instances, it may help to follow up in writing just to memorialize the understanding. Simple, right? You would be shocked how much potential energy is wasted in corporate America because people are afraid to get clear on things. Lack of clarity is a drain on people and organizations that is entirely preventable.

You will have ample opportunity in your life to perfect the skill of being clear and making clarity a personal trait. Start with yourself. Be honest with yourself. Slow down and think things through. Get grounded. Then think about others and the rest of the world. Think about how you engage others. Think about how you listen and talk to others. Do you speak up when you don't understand something? Do you ask others if they understand what you are sharing? Do you recognize situations where lack of clarity exists? When you order cookies, it might help to ask, "So when you say large cookies, exactly how big are they?"

Build these habits early and they will pay you dividends for the rest of your life.

Leading Practices

The world is moving so quickly these days. There are so many distractions that it seems achieving clarity may be nearly impossible! However, through all the noise, there are several best practices that can help guide us to maximize clarity for ourselves and those around us. Some of these are listed below:

- Communication Models and Media
- Culture of Clarity and The Six Thinking Hats®
- Clarity, Truth, and Integrity: Being Honest with Yourself
- Also see Active Listening Self-Assessment in *Listening* (Chapter 16)

Communication Models and Media

We can all work on our communication styles across different media and audiences to strive for clarity. The accepted communication model breaks down key important steps (Conway 2017):

- A sender encodes a message (through speech, text, chat, meme, song, etc.).
- Then sends it to a receiver who decodes it.
- Misunderstanding can result from "noise" coming from a variety of sources.
- Finally, the receiver provides feedback to the original sender.

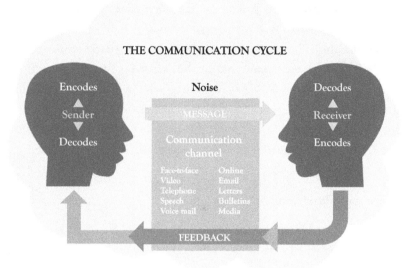

THE COMMUNICATION CYCLE

This basic model of communication is a starting point to ask yourself a few questions about each of these steps.

- Are we sending the right message?
- Are we utilizing the right media for this type of message?
- What noise could be present… that may degrade the core meaning/signal?
- What different kinds of feedback are we receiving?

Part of the challenge comes from the role of context in communication. Hall (1973) drew attention to the role of the situation in assessing communication effectiveness as the audience (or decoder) interprets the information they are receiving. Stay tuned not only to the sender/receiver but also the surrounding context. For example, the same message may be received very differently if you're in a high-stress versus low-stress situation; or to trusted colleagues versus a new team member. Also consider the role of the fundamental attribution error, which describes the tendency for us to blame others' character or personal flaws for their actions without taking into account external factors or the situation. You might think a person driving by you far too fast is a reckless jerk until you find out the driver's parent is in the emergency room.

Finally, the influence of technology on how we share information is also impacting how we communicate. We have so many choices that there is no one simple answer. What is most important is to be mindful and intentional about the type of communication channel you select for any specific message. The list of pros and cons in the table below provides a quick reference for selecting the best media to create the most clarity.

Culture of Clarity and Six Hats

In the Midwest United States, we are exceedingly "Nice." At least that's what we hear when others visit our region. We're generally described as helpful and neighborly. It could have something to do with the weather. Because if you must deal with the hottest summers and coldest winters, maybe we all need to work together to survive: It is us versus Mother Nature! Sometimes we even refer to a dominant culture of "Midwest Nice," which means we wouldn't say an unpleasant/critical word if it can be avoided. This is generally polite and pleasant, but it can create significant problems when direct communication is required. In sociology or psychology, our Midwest Nice may be the product of more collectivistic behaviors (rooted in rural agricultural traditions) rather than individualistic behaviors found more often in urban areas. Midwest Nice generally serves to preserve tradition and the status quo, which can also have devastating consequences when the status quo isn't fair, just, or legal.

Therefore, it is critical to understand your own culture and the influences it has upon you at an individual, team, organizational, and

Types	Description	Advantages	Disadvantages
Oral	Face-to-face communication including meetings, interviews, speeches, and presentations. F2F communication allows nonverbal cues and immediate feedback between sender and receiver. Oral communication is most appropriate when delivering bad, sensitive, or personal news.	• Provides opportunity for immediate feedback • Involves nonverbal cues • Allows for immediate feedback and consensus building	• Provides no permanent record of communication • Reduces sender's control of message • Immediate feedback may nor be constructive
Written	Written messages, other than digital, are used to communicate routine, day-to-day, information to audiences inside and outside of an organization. Memos, letters, reports, or proposals fall into this category.	• Provides permanent record • Shared easily with large audiences • Minimizes emotional reaction to message	• Delays feedback including nonverbal cues • Takes time and resources to distribute
Visual	Visual documents are communication formats in which one or more visual element play a central in conveying the message and are supported by small amounts of text. SlideDoc Reports and Infographic illustrations fall into this category.	• Conveys complex ideas • Simplifies messages • Reduces demand on receiver's time demand • Provides permanent record	• Requires specialized skills and more time to produce • Increases difficulty to transmit and store
Digital	Electronic media have largely replaced printed messages in many companies. Some degree of technical skills is required to use this category. Blogs, wikis, and websites fall into this category.	• Delivers messages quickly • Reaches large audiences • Provides interactive media • Provides permanent record	• Entails privacy and security risks • Requires specialized skill and time to produce

The advantages and disadvantages of the four categories of business communications (Business Communication Essentials 2016) community/cultural level. For instance, you may prefer a generally direct communication style, but the team, organization, and/or surrounding community may strongly exhibit indirect cultural norms. In this situation, you must find a way to achieve a culture of clarity that allows all viewpoints to be heard. One tool we've found that works exceptionally well for a group that isn't comfortable bringing healthy challenge is to explicitly assign a "devil's advocate" to raise questions and deliver hard truths. This concept is developed even more in Edward De Bono's (2021) model for clear and creative communication titled "The Six Thinking Hats®," which is summarized below.

- The White Hat calls for information known or needed. "The facts, just the facts."
- The Yellow Hat symbolizes brightness and optimism. Under this hat, you explore the positives and probe for value and benefit.
- The Black Hat identifies risks, difficulties, and problems. The risk management hat may be the most powerful hat, but could also be a problem if overused. This hat spots difficulties where things might go wrong and why something may not work. It is inherently an action hat that points out issues of risk with intent to overcome them.

White hat
Data, facts, information known or needed

Blue hat
Manage process, next steps, action plans

Red hat
Feelings, hunches, instinct and intuition

Yellow hat
Values and benefits, why something may not work

Black hat
Difficulties, potential problems, why something may not work

Green hat
Creativity, solutions, alternatives, new ideas

- The Red Hat signifies feelings, hunches, and intuition. When using this hat, you can express emotions and feelings and share fears, likes, dislikes, loves, and hates.
- The Green Hat focuses on creativity—the possibilities, alternatives, and new ideas. It's an opportunity to express new concepts and new perceptions.
- The Blue Hat is used to manage the thinking process. It's the control mechanism that ensures the Six Thinking Hats® guidelines are observed.

Finally, in this chapter about clarity we want to be very clear on this point: No communication style or culture is inherently good or bad. What is most important is to be able to recognize different communication styles and how best to achieve clarity within each.

Clarity, Truth, and Integrity: Being Honest With Yourself

In the famous movie *Liar Liar*, Jim Carrey plays a lawyer who had grown accustomed to lying to get what he wanted. One morning, he wakes up to find himself cursed to tell the truth and nothing-but-the-truth the entire day! With this radical honesty (a.k.a. clarity), he has hilarious struggles both personally and professionally.

Clarity doesn't necessarily mean saying out-loud anything that comes into your mind. Who knows, it may not even require 100 percent transparent honesty 100 percent of the time with others. However, we would suggest that being 100 percent honest with yourself is incredibly important to producing clarity with others. As we discussed previously, Sun Tzu and the ancient Greek's suggested that "Knowing Thyself" is the first step in achieving successful goals. By extension, by achieving a profound understanding of your own values, thoughts, and opinions you can express yourself more clearly to those around you.

This internal clarity also produces external integrity. By having solid internal foundations, your decisions and actions will be coherent and aligned. You can say with confidence, "Hell *yes!*", "I'm willing to do X, Y or Z," or a polite "No, thank you." When you don't have that internal clarity, you cannot hope to be clear for others.

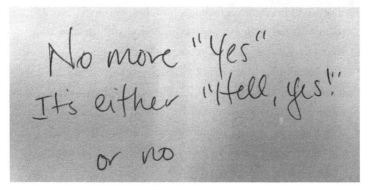

Note given to the author to help ensure commitment and select a few important priorities

Bonus Leading Practice

It can be very useful to "work through the problem" in advance to ascertain where you have clarity and where you do not. For example, if you're working on a big project, it is important to understand the project well enough to come with an opinion. The process of working through all the materials will help you anticipate what possible decisions or adjustments need to be made. With that initial investment/effort, you can then provide clear direction for yourself and others. We call it "sweating the problem." If you don't work through the problem first, then you cannot hope to be able to communicate about it clearly.

Shared Wisdom: Lessons From the Road

One of the best pieces of advice comes to us from history with the whimsical but very insightful comment from Blaise Pascal. It really does take more effort and focus to create a clear, crisp message!

I would have written a shorter letter, but I didn't have the time.

—Blaise Pascal
French Mathematician

Robert, a senior principal software engineer, shares how important it is to not only get things clear in your mind, but the additional challenge of creating a shared perspective.

Yes, it's obvious to you. But it's not obvious to anyone else. Unless you figure out how to make it obvious to everyone, you should learn to enjoy frustration.

I was told this long after I had become a senior engineer, when my organization had slammed face-first into yet another disaster that I had predicted and warned against.

—Robert Meegan, Senior Principal
SystemKnot LLC, California, USA

Craig, founder of a management consultant firm, shares his observation on how important it is to communicate your ideas as your career accelerates.

The biggest problem I have faced to date is my failure to communicate to my superiors my ideas, strategy, and intention to add value to an organization I most cherished working for. It's not a problem I was able to solve as at that time I had no mentor, grounding, or comprehension of the scale of the global strategy at hand. Those that I failed to collaborate/win over with were my managers/mentors, yet the challenge we all faced was that we were promoted into roles in a rapidly changing and growing organization which was very fluid. Our skills, my skills, understanding and capacity to eliminate "background noise" during this transformation led to my failure to continue in the organization. It has been a life-changing event which took me three years of personal self-help and professional counseling to appreciate and understand and learn from. Today I continue to work on improving myself.

—Craig Pretorius, Consultant
CAP Consulting, Australia

Sangeeta, a senior portfolio manager, shares the power of the advice she received about being clear about your career objectives and how important it is to figure this out before looking to others for help.

The best advice I received about my career is to be crystal clear on what do I want to do or want to be in my career. Don't seek a career advisor if you don't have that clarity instead look for a mentor, coach, or guide to help you in understanding your passion, values, and career goals. I received this advice when I was in my mid-career phase.

—Sangeeta Mehta, Senior Strategic Portfolio Manager
John Deere, Iowa, USA

Cleo, a retired sales and marketing executive who has founded his own strategic consulting firm, shares a construct he calls the "three Cs" that helped him bring a multifaceted approach to his career and with it invaluable clarity.

Be aware and always know the "Rule of Three's." When taking on a new role, always know and understand the three things that got you hired, the three things that will get you promoted, and the three things that will get you fired. This construct provides a multidimensional aspect of clarity of managing the vital few and prioritizes your efforts on what matters most for you and the organization from a 360-degree perspective.

—Cleophus (Cleo) Franklin Jr., Founder
Franklin Strategic Solutions, Texas, USA

Reflections: What's Your Story?

1. What are your main insights/takeaways from the chapter at this moment?

_____

_____

_____

_____

_____

_____

_____

_____

_____

2. What are one to three goals/intentions you would like to set for yourself?

_____

_____

_____

_____

_____

_____

_____

_____

_____

Going Further: Questions, Readings, and References

Discussion Questions

7.1   Tony shared the story of Denny Mills cookies—think about a time when lack of clarity cost you in your life. How can this experience help you in the future?

7.2   Many leaders spoke about the challenge of communication when it comes to how you think about an issue versus how others may think about the same issue. What one or two steps can you take to make sure your clarity is extended to others who need to know?

7.3   Matthew and Jeff talk about the "Six Hats" tool. Try to use this tool on an issue that is important in your life. How does that make you feel about the issue?

7.4   Situations matter when trying to communicate a topic to others. How can Hall's research and the pros and cons of different communication media help you improve your communication?

7.5   Think about a time when you didn't really understand what someone was saying to you. Did you do anything about it? Could you have handled it differently?

7.6   Think about a time when you were crystal clear about a certain issue. How did that clarity make you feel? What actions did you take? How did you communicate it to others?

Suggested Reading

Goulston, M. 2010. *Just Listen: Discover the Secret to Getting Through to Absolutely Anyone.* New York, NY: American Management Association.

Luntz, F. 2007. *Words That Work: It's Not What You Say, It's What People Hear.* New York, NY: Hyperion.

Sullivan. J. 2017. *Simply Said: Communicating Better at Work and Beyond.* Hoboken, NJ: Wiley.

References

Bovee, C.L., J.V. Thill, and J.A. Scribner. 2016. *Business Communication Essentials* (4th ed.). Don Mills, ON: Pearson Canada Inc.

Conway, K. 2017. "Encoding/Decoding as Translation." *International Journal of Communication* 11, p. 18.

de Bono, E. 2021. *Six Thinking Hats*, 2nd ed. New York, NY: Penguin Group.

Hall, S. 1973. "Encoding and Decoding in the Television Discourse." Discussion Paper. Birmingham, UK: University of Birmingham.

CHAPTER 8

Feedback

FEEDBACK

SHARING
RECEIVING
APPRECIATION
COACHING
EVALUATION

Feedback is the Breakfast of Champions.

—Ken Blanchard
American Author

Introduction

Feedback loops are all around us to help make life easier to navigate. Homes have thermostats that constantly measure room temperature, sending signals to the furnace or the air conditioner to keep the temperature comfortable. Our body fights off illness by raising our body temperature to drive out viruses and bacteria that harm our body if not contained. Sensors in the road are linked up to the streetlights to quickly enable you to travel further on our journey. The value of feedback loops is everywhere.

Being open to feedback in your career and more broadly how you run your life is critical for your personal development. Not only does it demonstrate humility and an earnestness to learn and grow, but it informs you about yourself in ways you cannot accomplish on your own. Receiving unvarnished and truthful feedback is one of the greatest gifts you will ever receive in your career. It may not feel like that at the time, but perhaps that is also when the dividends are the greatest. On the other hand, not being open to feedback could be a red flag to others, essentially telling them you are done growing.

Having someone give you feedback on your performance is one of the highest return investments you will ever have in your career. It's up to you how to use this investment.

Tony's Lessons From Personal Experience

"You know, Tony, people say you are kind of an odd duck too from time to time." This was the comment passed to me a little after 6 a.m. in the cafeteria of the John Deere assembly plant in Waterloo, Iowa. Every day I met with a couple friends first thing in the morning. We would prepare for the day ahead over a cup of coffee. I had just shared with the group that I thought it was odd how a coworker behaved at times in large meetings.

I remember being a bit struck by that direct input. I also remember how he smiled when he said it knowing that it might catch me off guard a little. As I thought about that moment several things came to mind:

- By my pointing out that our coworker was an "odd duck," I also sent a message that of course "I wasn't odd" at all.
- I also communicated to this employee that I perhaps was accustomed to making judgments about coworkers but only sharing them with a select few. Maybe I thought something strange or intriguing about everyone?
- By the look on my face, I most likely communicated that I wasn't used to getting that kind of direct feedback. And that was a correct assumption.

I think back to that conversation from time to time even though it happened over 13 years ago. It was such an awesome comment that represented a true investment he was making in me. I kind of became numb to what it was like to get real, honest, insightful feedback by that time in my career. By the time people had gotten to know me well enough to give me that kind of feedback, I'd usually already moved on to a new role. Moving from job to job in short succession does not provide a good closed-loop system for your personal development when it comes to feedback.

I kept in touch with that employee after he retired, and we got together every once in awhile for lunch to catch up. I believe that single comment he made cemented our friendship and elevated our working relationship. It showed me he cared enough to invest in me. He cared enough to share with me some balanced feedback at just the perfect moment. And he did it knowing that I would most likely be a bit surprised. What is really cool to me is that it was a totally spontaneous comment on his part—there was no way to anticipate the topic we were to discuss that morning. It was just a powerful moment and it stuck with me.

Feedback is truly fuel for your career if you are big enough to seek it out and accept the value it can create for you. Make it a habit in your early career to seek input from others. It shows you want to learn. It prevents you from developing bad habits. It demonstrates an attitude of lifelong learning. It only leads to good, even if people tell you that you have a ton of problems to iron out. It might even put you in a bad mood if people pile on. But think about it: What if people had that kind of input and didn't share it?! Pro tip—don't go overboard—focus on the task/job at hand and maybe ask for feedback once a year or during annual review time from your boss, people you interact with, or people you trust.

There is only one thing worse than getting negative feedback—not getting it!

Leading Practices

Our ability to learn and grow is partially dependent upon the feedback we receive from others. Ideally, we want to receive regular, constructive information from others so we can address any shortcomings and build upon our strengths. Even with the best intentions, however, these conversations can have unintended negative consequences. It is important to understand the following:

- Types of Feedback
- Approaches to Asking for Feedback
- Four-Step Model for Giving Feedback

Types of Feedback

According to Douglas Stone and Sheila Heen (2014), we can divide feedback into three types of communication:

- Appreciation—expressions of gratitude and recognition
- Coaching—sharing better ways to do something and helpful ideas for consideration
- Evaluation—here is how you did and where you stand compared to a standard

Awareness of these three modes is important not only because they allow you to ask for the kind of information you want, but also so you can consider how your own communication will be received. Appreciation tends to generate positive emotions and increased motivation. Coaching provides space to process emotions, build relationships, and improve skills. Evaluation is important but is also where there is the most risk for negative reactions. Ideally, appreciation and coaching precede evaluation over time. However, there is always a chance for someone to default to a mode that is not the most productive in a given moment, that is, sometimes you may receive evaluation when in actuality you want coaching. As discussed in the next section, attempt to phrase your questions to shape the response you want.

Approaches to Asking for Feedback

As a general rule, clear, simple, and direct requests will lead to better data and conversations. For example, saying to a colleague before a meeting, "After my presentation today, please tell me one thing that went well and one thing that I could improve, is that OK?" This request is going to get you specific, directional feedback that can be used to build additional skills. If you ask the more general, "how did that presentation go?" you're likely to get an evaluation though it may still be constructive.

It is not always easy to receive feedback. You may experience moments of anger or frustration in the communication. Negative emotions can stem from at least three factors: (1) you do not believe the information you're receiving is accurate, (2) the nature of your relationship with the person who is providing the feedback, and/or (3) the feedback clashes with your self-image or ideals, which in turn creates distress.

When feedback seems nonsensical, you should seek to understand it. Instead of rejecting it, ask the person to tell you more, provide an example, show you data, and so on. We are all subject to biases in our perceptions, and blind spots, which are shortcomings we fail to see in ourselves. One of the most powerful biases is called the fundamental attribution error (See discussion in Chapter 7). When we are making sense of behavior, we tend to use the environment or context to explain our own outcomes but tend to put too much emphasis on the individual when judging others' behavior. Imagine, for example, that someone speeds by you on the highway. You may initially assume the other person is reckless or irresponsible. If you were told that the person is headed to the hospital to see a very sick relative, however, then your perception changes based on contextual information. When you are given feedback that strikes you as off base, be open to learning why without immediately becoming defensive.

Is it easier to get hard feedback from a close friend, a professional colleague, or somebody you just met? Someone you like and respect or someone whom you feel is unqualified or does not really know you? Be aware of and endeavor to separate the "what" of the feedback and the "from whom" it is coming. If there are relationship issues to address, that conversation should be separate from the content of the feedback which could in fact be quite valuable regardless. See *Relationships* (Chapter 12) for more information on managing relationships.

Finally, as discussed in *Self-Image* (Chapter 1), our identities and selves are always evolving. If you receive feedback with a growth mindset, even negative portrayals and incidents become opportunities for learning and growth. Making a mistake at work does not make you an inherently bad person. After all, results also depend on factors such as luck. There is nothing wrong with experiencing anger or disappointment when events do not go as you would like or had planned, but strive not to dwell on them, and try to maintain your focus on what you can learn to improve.

As you move through your career, consider taking an intentional approach to obtaining feedback from your colleagues. Beyond providing insights to help you grow more quickly, having a partner in your development will help build better relationships at work and lead to greater satisfaction with your efforts at work. So, we encourage you not to rely solely on an annual review or similar exercise, build the habit of obtaining constructive conversations on a regular basis. To do so, consider the following:

- Decide what areas or topics you want to work on and then prioritize them. You cannot tackle everything at once so pick one or two which you think will have the biggest impact on your career. You may also think about choosing one that will give you a "quick win" and another that may be a little more difficult.
- Select one or two people whom you trust and respect to ask for feedback. Are they the right people for the topics you've chosen?
- What is the right cadence for your interactions? Is it in the context of daily activities, for instance, if you want to stop interrupting people, or is it an event like the creation of communication documents that may only occur from time to time?
- Prepare to receive the feedback—active listening, probing questions to clarify the information, avoiding defensive responses, and planning out next steps after the conversation with an expression of thanks.

Then, reflecting one of the consistent themes of this book, act! Put the feedback into practice and be sure to let your advisor(s) know what has happened and how you're doing. This will build in accountability and trust over time. See *Goals* (Chapter 6) for additional guidance on how to set goals with the information and reflections you receive.

Sharing Feedback

As you advance in your career, you will likely be called upon to provide feedback as well. We would also say that if you are going to ask for others to help you, you should be willing to reciprocate. The management book *The Leader Lab* provides us with a four-step model to consider when offering an evaluation (Luna and Renninger 2021).

1. Get the "micro" yes: Ask if you can share insight so the other individual is open and prepared to receive your perspective.
2. Provide data: Be as specific and objective as possible, try to focus on behaviors.
3. Share impact: Point out exactly how the behavior or event impacted those involved.
4. Question: Invite a reaction and set up a path of action toward with the listener.

This formula guides the listener toward action to learn and improve based on timely and directional advice. It can also create a feedback loop and build accountability.

Shared Wisdom: Lessons From the Road

Being self-aware is like a powerful mirror to your life and one that will help guide you no matter what your situation is. As our community of leaders share below, the power of feedback is the fuel for a successful career and personal growth.

A sales and marketing vice president in a consumer goods organization shares the value in identifying people who are willing to give you candid feedback.

> *Find people in the business who will provide you candid feedback on performance and behavior. It made a huge difference!*
> —Vice President, Sales and Marketing
> Consumer goods industry, USA

Todd, a senior executive of an agricultural foundation, shares a personal story about challenges he faced in his career and how powerful gaining the right type of feedback ultimately led to greater outcomes and personal growth.

Taking over a team of 10 that was already established. I came from the "outside" and didn't have their respect or street credibility. I started by showing them what I could do and outworking them. Slight mistake with good intentions. I realized that the more I did and the more I wanted to be deep into their work, I was unknowingly slowing us down. They saw me as competing with them, not leading. So they stopped bringing solutions to me. They just brought problems (monkeys), and sat back and waited on me to give them an answer. Which didn't win anyone over.

I overcame it by asking HR if they could coordinate an outside person to facilitate a 360 review of me. It was tough but so valuable. How I reacted was key. Acknowledge and thank them for being honest. I had to remain calm and not try and answer or disprove their comments. That was their personal view, not mine.

I picked just a few things to work on and openly shared that with them. I asked for their support and gave them permission to call it to my attention if I fell back into my old ways.

I also found out they wanted to understand how I made decisions, where they could have input, or when they could be involved versus when they just wanted me to make a decision. I had to be a better communicator in that respect. We agreed on criteria and I gave them freedom to make decisions under certain circumstances. It was invaluable in building trust.

The other important lesson from the 360 was that I had to guard against, "thinking out loud" and talking strategy with only one person on the team. I gained much more respect when I communicated to the entire team.

A year after the 360 it had turned around. We had NO staff turnover for four years. And our department consistently had the highest employee engagement survey ratings in the organization.

—Todd Greenwood, VP, Business Development
Farm Journal Foundation, Indiana, USA

Chris, a retired executive, shares how influential very direct feedback in the moment early in his career shaped his development and future success.

Early in my career one of my managers provided "very direct" feedback regarding my approach working with both dealers and customers. I was new in my role. With that, I was displaying a degree of overconfidence in my capabilities, and rather than serving both our dealers and customers in a support role, my overconfidence was causing me to become overly direct with my responses and in some cases even displaying a "cocky" behavior. As a result, my manager received feedback from a number of my dealers indicating they were displeased with my approach with both their employees and their customers. In addition, rather than serving as a teacher and mentor to our dealer technicians and assisting them in finding answers to problems, I would diagnose a problem and provide them the solution. This approach was in direct conflict to my role which was to assist them in finding the answers utilizing all processes and procedures. My manager pulled me aside and provided very strong coaching on how to approach my role and more importantly how to build and maintain positive, productive relationships with those I served. He was very direct and left a long-lasting impression on me as to how my behavior affects others. As a result, he coached me to address a behavior pattern that would have likely negatively impacted my career. Throughout my career, I utilized this coaching both as an employee and a manager of people to ensure I approached all relationships, roles, and responsibilities in the appropriate manner. I also used this example on numerous occasions with direct reports to provide coaching moments.

—Chris Ohnysty, Retired Executive
John Deere, Iowa, USA

Floyd, an executive coach and business consultant, shares how he's asked for unbiased feedback and how personally challenging, but rewarding, it can be when you truly receive it.

Over the years, there's been either a mentor or even many times clients who I've asked for unbiased feedback that helped me. A few times, I wouldn't say I liked it, but I heard it and responded. Many times we are inside our thoughts, and decisions become cloudy. As a leader, the goal is to make more right decisions than wrong. You have to be clear headed but also have quality information.

—Floyd Jerkins, Executive Coach
Jerkins Consulting, Florida, USA

A social innovator working on rural revitalization shares the power of identifying and addressing blind spots in our career. By definition, blind spots are parts of our behavior or performance that we ourselves cannot see, hence the need for feedback from others.

I was doing a role long-term because it was what was most needed in my department and I was good at it, but it didn't utilize my greatest strengths that fuel my passion. The real problem was that I didn't recognize or utilize my "superpowers" (which we all have). To avoid problems like that I learned to engage others to receive insights to discover and remediate my "blind spots" (which we also all have).

—Social Innovator
Rural and Urban Underserved, Iowa, USA

Reflections: What's Your Story?

1. What are your main insights/takeaways from the chapter at this moment?

_____

_____

_____

_____

_____

_____

_____

_____

_____

_____

2. What are one to three goals/intentions you would like to set for yourself?

_____

_____

_____

_____

_____

_____

_____

_____

_____

_____

Going Further: Questions, Readings, and References

Discussion Questions

8.1   Tony talked about the power of honest, genuine feedback he received from a trusted colleague. When is the last time you got real feedback that made a difference in your life? If you've never had this happen, did you take the time to thank that person for giving it to you?

8.2   Leaders consistently give credit to their success to people who have given them feedback over the years. Given how critical it is to receive honest feedback, how do you currently actively seek out input? What can you do immediately to seek feedback?

8.3   Matthew and Jeff talk about the power of three kinds of feedback: appreciation, coaching, and evaluation. Think about the feedback you have received in the past. Are you getting enough of the right kind of feedback you need, or do you need to ask for more directed feedback?

8.4   Think about a time when you received feedback you did not like to receive—the more difficult to receive the better. In retrospect, was it honest feedback, and did you handle it as well as you could have? Think about how you may react in the future to feedback that is difficult to receive and vow to do better each and every time.

8.5   From whom do you get feedback? Why? Are you getting a good mix from boss, coworker, and others who observe your work?

8.6   Do you give input to others? How do you invest in their development?

Suggested Reading

Harvard Business Review. 2014. *Giving Effective Feedback* (HBR 20-Minute Manager Series). Boston, MA: Harvard Business Review Press.

Huston, T. 2021. *Let's Talk: Make Effective Feedback Your Superpower*. New York, NY: Penguin Books.

Patterson, K., J. Grenny, R. McMillan, and A. Switzler. n.d. *Crucial Conversations: Tools for Talking When Stakes Are High*. New York, NY: McGraw-Hill.

Scott, K. 2017. *Radical Candor: Be a Kick-Ass Boss Without Losing Your Humanity*. New York, NY: St. Martin's Press.

References

Luna, T., and L. Renninger. 2021. *The Leader Lab: Core Skills to Become a Great Manager, Faster*. Hoboken, NJ: Wiley.

Stone, D., and S. Heen. 2014. *Thanks for the Feedback: The Science and Art of Receiving Feedback Well*. New York, NY: Penguin Books.

PART 3

How Will I Get There?

Teamwork, Decisions, Hard Work, Relationships, and Adversity

CHAPTER 9

Teamwork

TEAMWORK	TRUST
	COLLABORATION
	COMMITMENT
	COMMUNICATION

*The strength of the team is each individual member. The strength of
each member is the team.*

—Phil Jackson, Basketball coach

*Individual commitment to a group effort—that is what makes a team
work, a company work, a society work, a civilization work.*

—Vince Lombardi, American football coach

Introduction

There is tremendous value in personal fortitude and the power of individual contribution to any worthwhile cause. I'm constantly impressed by how much an individual can achieve in a single lifetime. The human will to accomplish things seems like an endless highlight reel of amazing life achievements—mountains climbed, roads run, waters swum, music played, and on and on and on. Human beings are designed for achievement, and it never ceases to amaze me what a single person can do on this planet.

But if you want to really achieve something spectacular and long-lasting, you need a *team*. Being part of a team will take you further, farther, and higher than you can ever do on your own. To do truly amazing things, you rarely, if ever, have all the cards you will need to play your life's greatest hand. Being able to excel in a team environment has never been more important than it is in today's modern world.

Tony's Lessons From Personal Experience

From a young age, we are taught about teamwork. For me it was with the family unit and how jobs were done around the house, planting and weeding the garden, and making meals. From there, sports came into my education with baseball, basketball, and football. All of these activities taught me to work hard to improve as an individual, but when on the job or on the field, it was all about the team and how I could work with others.

As my professional career started, it was clear to me that being a part of a team was central to value creation in such a large and complex company. I learned how to study the microstructure of steel from a skilled team in a metallurgy lab. I learned how to harden steel gears from the union workers on the shop floor. When things went wrong, I relied on the advice of many who went before me to show me the way. I learned how to lead a team by spending time with three shifts keeping parts flowing to the assembly line. I'll never forget the pressure to deliver quality parts at cost and on time, always in a safe environment and in a safe manner.

While books continue to influence me in major ways to accelerate my learning, my involvement with teams early in my career was instrumental in my development. Looking back, I realize what a gift it was to be a part of such teams at a relatively early age!

The earlier you realize that you are always part of a more complex structure the better. The key to sustainable value is working with others to build or create something bigger than yourself. The sooner you get experience being a part of a team, creating a team, leading a team, or fixing a broken team, the better off you will be. You may be great and have awesome capabilities, but they pale in comparison to what you can accomplish if you can work effectively with other people. Even if you are the greatest leader in the world, when you get to the mountain top, be sure you have your team with you.

Michael Jordan, Mia Hamm, Tom Brady, Simone Biles, Cristiano Ronaldo, and Wayne Gretzky are all awesome athletes, but they will be the first to tell you what propelled them was their team wins: How the team worked together and how they as leaders made the team better. You may not become as famous as these athletes, but hey, maybe you will. Either way, famous or not, the power of teamwork is the same for everyone!

Not getting this figured out early in your career can lead to a lot of problems. To begin with, first impressions are extremely hard to overcome. Sadly, in some cases, they never are overcome. Second, it can lead to people not investing in you. People are naturally turned off by people who think the world revolves around themselves. People stop helping you. They stop interacting with you. They may even avoid you. Often the derailing of a great career starts when people stop giving you feedback.

In worst-case scenarios, it leads to the worst of all performance comments: "he/she cannot work with others." *Don't be this person.* Find ways to work effectively with others. Seek team membership and affiliation. Invest in others and don't worry about who gets credit. Find ways to create value beyond yourself. "Out-collaborate" your peers.

You bring unique skills and capabilities to your daily life. You go to school and accumulate more and more experiences that carry you forward in life. What you aren't so good at, you can often find in others. What you are good at, you often enjoy sharing with others. Anytime you are working to accomplish a complex or difficult task or job, it often requires the talents of many to be successful (or some days just simply possible)!

How your talents combine with others is called teamwork. The power in the potential of your aspirations lies in how well you work with others. If you want to get the most out of life, it's something you have to master, so get started today!

Leading Practices

Throughout your career, it is likely that you will be working on or leading teams. Should you decide to get involved in community organizations, religious groups, or volunteer opportunities, you will also need to draw on team skills to accomplish your objectives. As such, it is worth establishing a baseline understanding of what typically constitutes high-performing teams as well as the common problems teams experience. With these two reference points in mind, you should be in a stronger position to understand team dynamics and become an effective member and leader of teams in various spheres of life.

- Being a Good Team Member
- Understanding Highly Effective Teams
- Diagnosing Team Dysfunction

Being a Good Team Member

Research from the Predictive Index (Silbert n.d.) summarizes five key aspects of being a good team member across contexts:

1. Flexibility—collaboration may require compromise to balance competing individual and group needs.
2. Active listening—engage with colleagues and invest energy into vetting their ideas.
3. Problem solving—think critically, generate solutions, and mediate conflict to constructive ends.
4. Effective communication—share information via channels that meet team needs. Understand the norms that govern when a face-to-face meeting is expected versus an e-mail versus a short text message.
5. Positivity—bring your enthusiasm to the task and celebrate the group's successes.

Reflect on your most recent team meetings. Were you actively listening and collaborating to reach the shared goals? Was any conflict constructive or destructive? Did you bring energy to help your teammates get enthused and tackle the agenda?

Understanding Highly Effective Teams

Whether written down or not, it is useful to recognize that all teams function on a framework sometimes called the "team contract." This is a shared understanding of how the team is going to operate, divide responsibilities, manage communication, track individual and team performance, resolve conflicts, and so on. In the absence of formal standards, listen for clues when you join a team for this type of information. The sooner you understand the norms that govern expectations for team members, the sooner you can contribute effectively to the team's goals and help it improve.

According to the Society for Human Resource Management, high-performing teams are characterized by the following:

- A deep sense of purpose and commitment to the team's members and to the mission
- Relatively more ambitious performance goals than average peer teams
- Mutual accountability and a clear understanding of members' responsibilities to the team and individual obligations
- A diverse range of expertise that complements other team members' abilities
- Interdependence and trust between members—even better if team members enjoy psychological safety, describing a situation in which the team is a safe space for interpersonal risk-taking, which Google's Project Aristotle found to be the most important characteristic of underpinning outstanding teams in its research (Doigg 2016)

This definition provides additional context into how you can be a good team member. Do you understand your team's why and reason for being? Are you contributing actively and effectively to the desired outcome? Do you know your role? Are you learning so you can support other members and fill any gaps in the group's knowledge?

Diagnosing Dysfunction

While we would prefer to work on great teams, the complexity of teams and human relationships can lead to dysfunctional teams as well. In his 2002 book *The Five Dysfunctions of a Team*, Patrick Lencioni described five key hurdles to achieving a high-performing team.

If you find yourself on a team that is not working well, the dysfunctions provide you a path toward improving the team (see the figure on the following page). The behaviors recommended next to each dysfunction indicate what you can do to help mitigate their influence on your team and in the organizations to which you belong.

Shared Wisdom: Lessons From the Road

Entire books are dedicated to the concept of teamwork and how important it is to business, careers, and the world in general when it comes to solving important, complex problems. Our experts share freely how critical this is to build a strong career and a more fulfilling life. Rarely do we ever hold all the cards in our own hand to do what is truly necessary, or to optimize the solutions to the challenges we face.

Mark, a director of international finance, shares the power of teamwork in working through an existential crisis during the 2008 financial crisis. While he faced immense challenges, he notes the value of having a strong team, and while the hard work was challenging, the experience was also very rewarding.

> *I was Director of Corporate Finance during the 2008–2009 credit crisis. I was responsible for our bank relationships and credit rating agency relationships, in addition to corporate finance decisions. We needed to remain funded during a time of limited liquidity, to have contingency planning and execution as banks imploded, and to keep our credit rating from getting downgraded. In one word, the key was TEAMWORK. We had an "all-hands-on deck" mentality with the subject matter experts,*

DYSFUNCTIONAL TEAMS

- Poor performance and results
- Team turnover

- Missed deadlines and key deliverables
- Poor performance is tolerated and creates environment of resentment and hopelessness

- Ambiguous direction and priorities
- Revisit discussions again and again
- Absenteeism

- Go around problems
- Do not confront tough issues or behaviors
- Lack of transparency drives confusion

- Hesitate to ask for help
- Conceal weaknesses
- Dread meetings and avoid team members

INATTENTION TO RESULTS

AVOIDANCE OF ACCOUNTABILITY

LACK OF COMMITMENT

FEAR OF CONFLICT

ABSENCE OF TRUST

HIGH PERFORMANCE TEAMS

- Extraordinary and recurring performance, team-based results
- Highly motivated team

- Poor performers are managed and held accountable
- Same standards apply to everyone

- Buy-in and alignment on common objectives
- Clarity on direction and priorities
- Highly engaged team members

- Confront problems and issues quickly
- Develop practical solutions
- Get input from all team members, minimal politics

- Safe environment to speak up
- Team members help each other
- Leverage strengths for the team

and leveraged experts from banking partners, universities, and peer companies. We had a common goal (keeping the company solvent) and all worked together to do whatever it took to make sure that happened. It was a lot of work, but at the same time very rewarding and fun.

—Mark Halupnik, Director International Finance
John Deere, Illinois, USA

Jim Kouzes, author and leadership expert, shares how powerful it was to hear "you can't do it alone" early in his career and how important this advice was and continues to be for his career.

"You can't do it alone." I recall hearing this about 10 years into my career, but I bet I heard it earlier and didn't attend to it as much as I should early on. Looking back, though, this is absolutely the BEST advice I was given. I now share it with anyone who asks me this question.

—Jim Kouzes, Author, *The Leadership Challenge*,
Dean, Leavey School of Business
Santa Clara University, California, USA

Alex, a marketing and business development executive, shares his advice on how important it is to understand different perspectives and always try to understand others' perspectives when overcoming obstacles. Noteworthy is his observation that personal change and deeper introspection are often required.

The constant obstacle is cultural... even with co-nationals there will always be a different interpretation and different perspective, let alone when living and working abroad. One needs to understand that each person's mind and background is different, and therefore we need to take the other party into account. Unilateral decisions are not good, not for the short nor for the long term. Collaboration means finding solutions that would satisfy all parties. Every time I wish to be understood, I come to realize that is me who needs to realize something about the others.

—Alejandro Galindo, Regional Sales Director
Valeo, Queretaro, Mexico, USA

Kevin, a retired senior HR executive turned associate professor, shares powerful advice about the value in being a good teammate and not worrying about who gets the credit.

Being a good teammate and not worrying about who gets the credit for attaining strong results is part of a strong personal brand. I received this feedback early on, like in the first 5 years.

—Kevin Keith, Associate Professor
University of Iowa, Iowa, USA

Chris, an attorney and managing partner of a law firm, shares his advice around rallying earlier to recognize the power of teams and playing to others' strengths.

Recognizing the power of teams and collaboration sooner—you can accomplish so much more working with others and playing to everyone's strengths.

—Chris Sackett, Managing Partner/Attorney
BrownWinick Law, Iowa, USA

A chief technology officer of a start-up in Silicon Valley suggests success is measured by team, not individual, accomplishments.

Your success is measured when the team succeeded. In the middle of my career.

—Chief Technology Officer
Digital Start-Up, California, USA

Mike, a senior executive in the financial services industry, notes that as your career advances to more senior roles, the importance of teamwork and working with others will increase.

As you progress through your career in leadership roles, you'll quickly find you cannot "out work" your way through times of challenge and crisis. Rather, you need to rely on the skills and experience of others in your leadership. Received it from a mentor five years into my 24-year career.

—Mike Sheehy, Director of Global Fintech Partnerships
John Deere Financial, Iowa, USA

Ricardo, a retired senior executive in the financial services industry, shares one of the biggest challenges of his career was overcome by teamwork, collaboration, empowerment, trust, and respect.

I'm in general terms a very positive person and I always tried to see challenges as opportunities rather than problems. I would say that probably one of the biggest challenges I faced in my career was managing the business in Argentina during one of the most severe crises in that country (2001–2003). During that time, we needed the whole team's support and hard work, so I empowered every one of my team members, I showed to them my trust and respect to their job, to their opinions and suggestions. Additionally, I acted as facilitator of the team and made sure everyone in the team had very clear understanding of our mission, vision, goals, and the importance of the "how." At the end of the crisis, we accomplished our goals and objectives, and our unit/company became stronger than ever. Looking back, it is now easy to see that it was all about collaboration, teamwork, empowerment, trust, and respect, it was all about people, and how to get the best out of each one of the team members in an extremely difficult time for the country, the people, and our company.

—Ricardo Leal, Retired Executive
John Deere, Brazil

Brent, a senior executive with experience in start-ups as well as Fortune 100 companies, shares his experience on the importance of building a strong team, hard work, and giving the team the right support.

Building the Xchange Leasing business for Uber is the greatest challenge I've faced in my career so far. In general, I feel like business builds/start-ups are capstone experiences requiring an entrepreneur to bring strengths from several different domains to have a shot at success, and to have the self-knowledge/humility to know where your weaknesses are and a willingness to surround yourself with those who can help you plug them. In this case, some combination of aggressive recruiting/building a great team, giving those great people the resources/support to run, and lots of hard work were the three biggest elements that got us through that first year.

—Brent West, General Manager of Ford Commercial Solutions

Ford Motor Company, California, USA

Chad, president and COO of a major publishing firm, shares his challenges he faced when the team fell short of their potential and how he approached resolving the issues.

Dealing with a management team that didn't like each other and couldn't trust each other. Started teambuilding and slowly weeding out the weak links when it became obvious they did not want to make it work. (Five Dysfunctions of a Team provided a good starting point, Good to Great provided a good goal and pathway.)

—Chad Chandlee, President and COO

Kendall Hunt Publishing, Iowa, USA

Reflections: What's Your Story?

1. What are your main insights/takeaways from the chapter at this moment?

_____

_____

_____

_____

_____

_____

_____

_____

_____

2. What are one to three goals/intentions you would like to set for yourself?

_____

_____

_____

_____

_____

_____

_____

_____

_____

_____

Going Further: Questions, Readings, and References

Discussion Questions

9.1 Tony talked about how he learned about being a good teammate while on the job. When have you been a part of a high-performing team? How did it make you feel?

9.2 Many leaders have looked back on critical moments in their career and given credit to their success to being part of a high-performance team. What have your experiences on teams been so far in your life? How do the good experiences and the negative experiences inform you about your future experiences?

9.3 Of the five key aspects of being a positive team member (flexibility, active listening, problem solving, effective communication, and positivity), how do you think you are doing at the moment? What can you do to get better?

9.4 What does team trust mean to you? How can you make team trust stronger as a member of a team?

9.5 What was your greatest personal achievement in your life? Who helped you get there?

Suggested Reading

Coyle, D. 2018. *The Culture Code: The Secrets of Highly Successful Groups.* New York, NY: Bantam Books.

Gordon, J. 2018. *The Power of a Positive Team: Proven Principles and Practices That Make Great Teams Great.* Hoboken, NJ: Wiley.

Katzenbach, J.R., and D.K. Smith. 2006. *The Wisdom of Teams: Creating the High-Performance Organization* (Collins Business Essentials). New York, NY: HarperCollins.

Maxwell, J. 2002. *The 17 Essential Qualities of a Team Player: Becoming the Kind of Person Every Team Wants.* Nashville, TN: Thomas Nelson Publishers.

McChrystal, S., T. Collins, D. Silverman, and C. Fussell. 2015. *Team of Teams: New Rules of Engagement for a Complex World.* New York, NY: Portfolio.

References

Doigg, C. February 25, 2016. "What Google Learned from Its Quest to Build the Perfect Team." *New York Times Magazine.*

Lencioni, P. 2002. *The Five Dysfunctions of a Team: A Leadership Fable.* San Francisco, CA: Jossey-Bass.

Silbert, D. n.d. *5 Qualities of a Great Team Player.* www.predictiveindex.com/blog/team-player

Society for Human Resource Management. 2016. *Developing and Sustaining High-Performance Work Teams.* www.shrm.org

CHAPTER 10

Decisions

DECISIONS

ASK
ANALYZE
ANNOUNCE
ACT
ASSESS

In any moment of decision, the best thing you can do is the right thing. The worst thing you can do is nothing.

—Theodore Roosevelt
26th U.S. President

Introduction

The key to any significant accomplishment is the need to do your research. You must assess as much input as you can possibly render to give you the best understanding of every facet of the situation. You must apply the best analytics to take advantage of relevant data. You must apply all of your previous experience. You must consult experts to learn from their experience as well. To do something incredible and achieve great accomplishments, you need to do all of this in a timely manner. All of this, and one more thing: *You must make a decision.* And remember—not acting is still a decision.

You will make hundreds of thousands of decisions in your lifetime. Many decisions will be made within one day, while others will be made only once in a lifetime. Understanding the importance of making decisions and taking this responsibility seriously early in your career will help you in many ways. Every decision you make will be an opportunity to learn in many ways. Earlier in life, the decisions may seem critical but often in hindsight they are not. As you get practiced and confident in making decisions, the more consequential ones come later in life.

Make sure you use your decision-making skills to propel your life forward.

Tony's Lessons From Personal Experience

The most impactful development activity in my career involves making decisions. Making a decision and sticking around long enough to live with the consequences is a great way to learn. I wish I could say all of the decisions I have ever made were great decisions, but they weren't. I learned later in my life that you have to make decisions and just know that they aren't all going to produce great results. But nevertheless, sometimes you simply need to make a decision and press on.

I remember really having a hard time with an employee performance issue that I thought could result in a termination. Kerrie Keeler, a sales branch manager, gave me some great advice at the time. "If it doesn't bother you a little bit to fire someone, you shouldn't be in the job. In addition, if you can't make the call, you shouldn't be in the position." In that one discussion, I learned that it's OK to have a heart and feel bad about a difficult decision, but I also had the responsibility to move the organization forward. In the end, I learned in a lot of these situations it's better for the affected employee as well as the company in the long run, however unpleasant it is in the short term.

Another situation I faced many times was when someone would ask me, "So, where you are on this issue?" Sometimes it involved people I respected standing on opposite ends of an issue that I held the final say on or had substantial influence on. For example:

- How do you allocate tractor production between regions when demand is skyrocketing in every region and you have a limited production capacity in the factory?
- Will we enter a niche tractor market, and if so, exactly how?
- Should we adopt an agile operating model in one of our most strategic business units, and if so, exactly how?
- Should you take that job to broaden your experience even though you have to move, it is for lower pay, and there are no guarantees what would come next?
- Should we let go of someone who has a history of poor performance, or should we give them "one more chance," or what they used to call, "one more for the arbitrator"?

In all of these situations, I had to make a decision. Barry Schaffter, a retired senior officer of Deere & Company who I had the privilege of knowing for 30 years and working for twice in my career, told me once how important it is to make a decision as a leader. He advised me that

80% of the time you will make the right decision, and the 20% of the time it is wrong the organization will let you know. You just have to have the smarts and the will to make the best decision you can at the time, and the maturity and humility to know that you will be wrong sometimes and be smart enough to listen to your people and respond to them accordingly, in a timely manner.

He gave me this advice the first time I worked for him about 10 years into my career. I had accepted the lead marketing role for our precision agriculture unit, and it was the first time I had a global team to lead. I look back on that advice, at that very moment in my career, and believe to this day it helped me be a better leader from that day on. It was great advice because as a young leader in a highly visible role you don't want to make any mistakes. Barry knew that, and he also knew it would be a problem for me if I was unable to make decisions.

No matter where you are on your leadership journey you will need to develop a relationship with the decisions you make. I would encourage you to be very thoughtful about this and to make it a regular part of your career development. Think about the decisions you make from time to time. Ask others how you are doing, see *Feedback* (Chapter 8) for more information on soliciting feedback.

Leading Practices

Some important aspects of decision making are:

- Types of Decisions
- Decision-Making Models
- Common Biases

Decisions

Throughout every day, we are making thousands of decisions (Latham 2015). Many of them are nearly automatic and are referred to as programmed decisions. You get up, brush your teeth, maybe get some exercise, make a cup of coffee, and so on. Making sure you are comfortable with the decision rules you're following in your routine is important because many outcomes in life depend on the accumulated results of all these small choices.

Large, important decisions typically fall outside of our daily program. They are unprogrammed, and as such, garner more of our active attention and can lead to stress and anxiety. A large purchase, a long-distance move, changing careers, pursuing more education, or having a child are all examples of these kinds of decisions. Depending on how much information you have, your prior experience in similar situations, and the importance of the decision, there are different techniques you may employ to get you from reflection to action.

Again, it is important to realize that your overall quality of life depends on the quality of the decisions you make over time.

Decision Models

While there are many approaches to making decisions, let us consider four main ways. These four vary based on the relative importance of the choice, the amount of information available at the outset of the process, and how much time and energy you have to invest (Ireland and Miller 2004).

If asked to describe how a decision is made, most people will describe the linear process typical of the rational model. The problem or opportunity is identified, success criteria chosen, different alternatives are evaluated to find the best one, followed by implementation and evaluation. This description assumes we understand the decision, know our choices, and can optimize the outcomes.

Our principal problem with the rational model is the effort required to get to the decision both in gathering data, investigating alternatives, and the time involved. In 1978, Herbert Simon won the Nobel Prize in Economics in part for his assertion that most of time we "satisfice." In essence, we only pursue the model until a "good enough" alternative is found. This implies that we are not always seeking the very best outcomes and may try to solve several partly contradictory goals at the same time. All decision makers are trying to find satisfactory solutions to their own set of problems while considering how peers are solving theirs.

When we are faced with a situation that is very unfamiliar or no clear alternatives exist, we tend to pursue a more creative approach to making decisions. This can include activities like brainstorming or envisioning brand-new possibilities to solve a problem. Recently, the advent of design thinking has formalized a more robust methodology for creative problem-solving.

Finally, some experts estimate nearly 80 percent of all business decisions are made based on gut feeling. This is typically called the intuitive model of making decisions. This model is completely appropriate when time is very limited, the stakes are somewhat low, and you have prior experience upon which to base your choice.

In the workplace, the process could also incorporate a degree of scenario analysis, for instance:

- Compile the main business goals that will be impacted by the decision.
- Create three to four realistic alternatives and the success criteria for each one.
- Summarize what you know and what you don't know.

Model	Use this model when:
RATIONAL	• Information on alternatives can be gathered and quantified. • The decision is important. • You want to maximize your outcome.
BOUNDED RATIONALITY	• The minimum satisfactory criteria are clear. • You do not have, or you are not willing to invest, much energy and time into making the decision. • You are not trying to maximize your outcome.
INTUITIVE	• You have sufficient experience with the problem. • Due to time pressure, too much analysis would be costly. • Information may not be readily available. • Optimal goal may be unclear.
CREATIVE	• You are facing a new challenge or opportunity. • Solutions are not clear and need to be created from scratch. • You have time to immerse yourself in the issues.

- Write down what's likely to happen in the future, good and bad.
- Involve a team of at least two to six other stakeholders for feedback and revision.
- Write down what was decided, why, and who was involved.
- Implement the decision and schedule follow-ups to check-in on results.

Common Biases

We would like to think that we are rational beings who make decisions to maximize the benefit or value creation. However, studies show again and again that emotions, immediate context, past experiences, and other factors all impact how we approach problem-solving (Soll, Milkman, and Payne 2015). While this is not an exhaustive list, here are some common biases encountered when individuals make decisions, namely, confirmation, anchoring, halo effect, and overconfidence.

- *Confirmation bias*: This occurs when we seek out and retain data, evidence, or facts that confirm our previously held beliefs, actively ignoring or discounting any evidence in support of other conclusions or outcomes. It is the idea that we see what we want to see, and as such, we will filter information to reinforce our position.

- *Anchoring bias*: An overweighted focus or reliance on single piece of information or prior experience, often the first one we find, to make our subsequent judgments. Once you have set an anchor, your ability to accurately interpret new, potentially relevant information, is lessened. This is complicated by the impact of recency and salience on how individuals interpret information as we are likely to anchor on an item we just learned if it is familiar, interesting, or shocking. Consider how you would handle the dismaying testimony of the first witness in a case if the following four were boring but provided contradictory evidence.

- *The halo effect*: The influence of an overall impression of another individual or product on our judgment about its overall nature even if the activities in question are unrelated. For example, the belief that a star athlete could also be a great corporate leader. Most people are also more likely to believe the information coming from a boss they like rather than one they hate even if it is the same message.

- *Overconfidence bias*: This happens when a person overestimates their ability when making judgments due to perceived ability, past performance, or likelihood of success. This is akin to assuming that beating a team at the beginning of the season means you'll win again at the end while ignoring anything that changed during the intervening period.

It is nearly impossible to avoid all bias when you are making decisions and solving problems. However, an awareness of what they are does allow you to anticipate and attempt to mitigate the negative impacts they can have on the choices you make. For example, if you are concerned one or more of these biases are happening, you can try to seek out contradictory viewpoints, reframe the issue or question into scenarios or "what if…." questions, ask "why?" five times, or incorporate uncertainty and likelihood into how you talk about ideas.

Shared Wisdom: Lessons From the Road

Decisions will propel us and the world forward. Our community of experts had plenty of advice to share about this topic.

Dan, a retired aerospace engineer, shares the importance of critically evaluating career opportunities and making decisions carefully as they may not always be there for you in the future.

Opportunities arise during your career; you need to evaluate them carefully because I believe you will only get five good career-changing opportunities in your lifetime. I passed on my first one, and I think that would have been a great opportunity to move and start a new business office for the company.

—Dan Hausman, Aerospace Engineer (Retired)
Pratt Whitney Rocketdyne, Florida, USA

Jeff, a biology professor and executive director of a statewide STEM council, shares his simple but powerful advice when faced with a decision to make.

At a fork in the road, which way's right? Take input of those most trusted, combine with gut.

—Jeff Weld, Executive Director, Governor's STEM Advisory
Council
Iowa STEM Advisory Council, Iowa, USA

Jena, a General Manager at John Deere, shares how decisions and risk-taking have helped her in her career.

Whether on purpose or by accident, all of my career decisions have enabled me to build experiences that have led to new and fulfilling opportunities. I have taken risks in my career whether that was taking a lateral or "red circle/down grade" or changing industries (cosmetics to heavy equipment) or moving to India (a place many were unsure of going). My guidance to others is, and will continue to be, that taking career risks is worth it.

—Jena Holtberg-Benge, General Manager
John Deere Reman, Missouri, USA

Randy, senior executive in a consulting firm, shares valuable advice about making decisions sooner and about the need to "go with your gut." Also noteworthy is also his advice to have a bias for action.

There are several career decisions I would change if I could. In most cases, I would have made the same decision, but I would have made it a lot sooner. Early in my career, I would wait until I was 95%+ certain before I finally pulled the trigger. Now, I want to be 80% certain, and I then I go with my gut. My advice: Have a bias for action. Gather data, talk to others, make the decision, move out, then course correct as needed.

—Randy K. Kesterson, Executive / Advisor
North Carolina, USA

Mary Beth, a high school volleyball coach, expounds on the challenges of making player decisions in building her teams.

The biggest problem I have had is identifying players that don't help our team move in a positive direction. I have always wanted to surround our players with teammates that wanted to compete and unselfishly share their talents each day to make the team better. Some athletes are very talented, but have a bad work ethic, or are disrespectful to teammates and coaches.

There are times in my coaching career where we had to choose to not have an athlete on the team because the team's synergy would be stronger without her even though she was a good volleyball player. Those decisions are hard to make because you still like the athlete and you know that your decision as a coach will affect her greatly. But coaches need to remember that your decision also will positively affect the other 15 girls that make the team. It will also affect the direction that your team and program goes.

As a head coach at Dowling Catholic, I have always taken pride in selecting the right people who wear the Dowling Catholic volleyball jersey. We are constantly looking for the talented volleyball players who also have good attitudes, work hard, and are a great teammate. I know this is one factor that has made us a winning program and a state tournament team for the past 10 years.

—Mary Beth Wiskus, Head Volleyball Coach
Dowling Catholic High School, Iowa, USA

A general manager of a major factory shared the power of a mentor when dealing with sensitive issues related to your boss, as well as the wisdom of making decisions sooner rather than later.

A time when I was not aligned with my boss and we were trying to solve some challenging problems. A good mentor was very supportive to me and a great thought partner to help get me through it. My family is incredibly supportive. Other challenge was when I had two brilliant performers that were diametrically opposed as to how to solve a problem and could not come to consensus. I spent way too long trying to get them there and, in the end, had to pick one. I should have done that early on.

—Factory General Manager
John Deere, USA

Marco, a founder and managing director of a consulting firm, advises us to not look back after deciding even if things don't turn out exactly how we thought it would.

Once you have decided on your career next move don't look back! Engage with all you will to make it successful, even though it might not turn out as you expected.

—Marco Ripoli, Founder and Director
Bioenergy Consultoria, Brazil

A senior executive in a major automotive firm shares an intimate story about making personnel decisions that proved to be correct in the long term, but very challenging for the team and for the executive in the short term.

Perseverance and determination are foundational to weathering the challenges one faces during their career and mine are no different. I have had two periods where I felt I had hit a brick wall. The first occurred when I took over managing a specialized department. The outgoing leader was charismatic and loved. Although he wasn't the first manager of this department, I credit him with making it successful. Unfortunately, when I came in, I observed infighting and dysfunction within my managers. The individuals in question were both high performers but didn't work well together and created anxiety within the department. This was unacceptable to me. To remedy this situation, I had to make difficult personnel-related decisions that would create change while not effectively destroying anyone's careers. Initially my actions were met with mixed feedback because I upset the status quo. At the time, I was constantly questioning my decision, but I didn't let anyone around me see my insecurity. Looking back, I am 100% confident I took the right actions.

—Senior Executive
Major auto manufacturer, Michigan, USA

Jim, a retired executive in the financial services industry, shares great advice he received early in his career around the power of building a strong team and then giving the team the power to do their best work.

As I became a manager for the first time, my boss at the time told me that the most important decisions I will ever make in business would be putting the right people in the right chairs and letting them manage their areas of responsibility.

—Jim Israel, President (Retired)
John Deere Financial, Iowa, USA

Ralf, a professor of international management, shares his personal challenge in making people-related decisions and how helpful it was to have a good mentor at that phase of his career.

The first dismissal of an employee was an incredibly hard decision. I was lucky to have a great mentor at that time and the discussions were extremely helpful.

—Ralf Lanwehr, Professor of International Management
University of Applied Sciences Sudwestfalen, Germany

Reflections: What's Your Story?

1. What are your main insights/takeaways from the chapter at this moment??

_____

_____

_____

_____

_____

_____

_____

_____

_____

2. What are one to three goals/intentions you would like to set for yourself?

_____

_____

_____

_____

_____

_____

_____

_____

_____

_____

Going Further: Questions, Readings, and References

Discussion Questions

10.1　Tony talked about the need to get good at making decisions in his career. Think about the last decision you had to make. How intentional were you in how you approached it?

10.2　Many leaders talk about difficult decisions they had to make. Think about the most difficult decision you have made in your life. What made it so difficult, and in looking back, how do you think about that decision now?

10.3　Matthew and Jeffrey talk about the value of a step-by-step situational analysis while making a decision. Try to use this process on a current decision or go through a previous decision with this model and analyze what could have changed. What did you learn from this process?

10.4　What are your most influential biases? If you believe you have no biases, perhaps you have a bias toward overstating your capabilities.

10.5　Think about a time someone important to you made a decision you disagreed with or had a substantial negative impact on you. How did you feel about it?

10.6　Think back 5 to 10 years and reflect on how you made decisions then, versus how you do so today. Have you changed the process in any way, and if so, how and why?

Suggested Reading

Gladwell, M. 2005. *Blink: The Power of Thinking Without Thinking*. New York, NY: Little, Brown and Company.

Heath, C., and D. Heath. 2013. *Decisive: How to Make Better Choices in Life and Work*. New York, NY: Crown Business.

Kahneman, D. 2011. *Thinking, Fast and Slow*. New York: Farrar, Straus, and Giroux.

References

Ireland, R.D., and C.C. Miller. 2004. "Decision Making and Firm Success." *Academy of Management Executive* 18, pp. 8–12.

Latham, A. November 2015. "12 Reasons Why How You Make Decisions Is More Important Than What You Decide." *Forbes.*

Soll, J.B., K.L. Milkman, and J.W. Payne. 2015. "Outsmart Your Own Biases." *Harvard Business Review* 93, no. 5, pp. 64–71.

CHAPTER 11

Hard Work

HARD WORK

MOTIVATION
SACRIFICE
DISCIPLINE
COMMITMENT
ENERGY

You put in the time and the sweat for the satisfaction of knowing you've thrown yourself into the struggle. And you do it to make sure that if somebody does give you that opportunity you have been dreaming about, that you're worthy of it.

—Nick Nurse
Head Coach of Toronto Raptors

Introduction

Sometimes it's helpful to look at life through the lens of what we can or cannot control. Some things are simply out of our reach like how other people behave and what other people think. Expending energy on people and issues that are not under our control can be a distraction and a tremendous waste of time. Focusing on what you can control is infinitely more productive.

One of the most important things you can control is how hard you work.

The truth is, you can have outstanding personal attributes, a healthy body, a strong mind, and a great plan, but in the end, you will still fail if you don't have the will to work hard to succeed. Once you realize it's a choice you have to make, the world gets much easier to understand. Once you develop the attitude to do the homework necessary to succeed in all you do, you will accomplish more than you ever thought possible.

Do you want to set yourself up for success in all conditions you may face? Commit to working harder than anyone else and your odds of success will increase. Doing this over and over will build a lifetime of character and grit that you will be proud of.

Tony's Lessons From Personal Experience

Growing up there is "work" and then there is "hard work," and as a kid you learned to know the difference. Cleaning the dishes, mowing the lawn, shoveling snow, or if you grew up on a farm, there were always a million chores to do. And then there is *real work*. Chores might be good for allowance, but real work was something you got paid to do. For me, my first introduction to real work was detasseling corn for seed companies in western Iowa.

"Detasseling" is simply the act of removing the tassel, or top, of the corn plant. To create the right varieties of corn seed, male and female corn plants are planted next to each other, and the "tassels" of the female plants have to be manually removed to ensure the right pollination would occur. To accomplish this, every single female plant has to have the tassel removed. Kids from all over the Midwest do this for their summer jobs. For me, it will forever be etched in my memory as my first experience of real work.

Imagine waking at 5 a.m. to get on a bus at 5:30 to get to the fields by 6:30. You and a crew of other kids between ages 13 and 18 enter the field a little after dawn with the plants still wet with dew and begin walking in the rows pulling tassels off plants in half-a-mile long rows. Immediately you are drenched, and your hands start to wrinkle up. Just for kicks about one in every 20 tassels is full of bugs, spiders, or decayed in some way. When you get done with the first pass at the end of the field, you turn around and head back in for the second stretch after which you get a small break and a drink of water. About mid-day, the sun is high in the sky and what was drenching you in the morning now has turned into a sauna. You can barely breathe between the rows because it's so hot and humid. The corn plants are now sharp as razors and they cut your forearms until they bleed. You keep going, pulling thousands of tassels off in half-a-mile rows, and at some point, someone says enough is enough and we're done for the day. Nobody remembers the ride home because most of the time we are sleeping from pure exhaustion. Then it's back at it the next day.

It was incredibly hard work for a kid of 14 when I think about it. I hated it at the time, but today I realized it taught me a lot. I learned a sense of teamwork and met good kids from all over the county during those summers. I learned how awesome a jug of cold water, a ham sandwich, and Snack Pack pudding can taste after a morning of hard work. I learned some people complain and others just get it done. I wanted to be one of the ones who just got it done.

When I started my career, I began as a chemical engineer and later served four years as a shop-floor supervisor for a large John Deere factory in Waterloo, Iowa. I remember waking up in my car at 6 a.m. in the parking lot not knowing how I got there. I had been working 12+ hours days six days a week and had entirely lost track of time. I poured myself into the job and never worked harder in my life.

We all have our own version of what hard work is in our childhood and in our early parts of our career. At some point, we are confronted with discovering the difference between chores and work. First, there is the difference between "work" and "hard work." Then, I believe there is also a "work ethic" we learn at some point in our lives and that ethos sticks with us much beyond childhood. This work ethic says that you aren't afraid of working hard, but that you also have a committed attitude: you're totally cool putting in the time and energy to get a job done!

Develop a work ethic and don't be afraid to work hard in your career. It is entirely something you can control, and it can differentiate you from the rest of the world who may not have the work ethic you have.

Leading Practices

Hard work is very personal by its very nature. Some view hard work as putting in the hours and being fearless about what you are willing to sacrifice to get a difficult task completed. Others will view hard work not so much as personal sacrifice of sweat and effort as much as "work smarter, not harder." Some will interpret hard work as a type of core value as in "she has a Midwest work ethic" or "he was raised on a dairy farm, so they are not afraid of hard work."

Hard work is very personal by its very nature.

No matter how you view hard work there are certain elements that can be helpful in building a strong foundation for a successful career and a more fulfilling life. By no means an exhaustive list, presented below are five principles we believe will help ensure you have all the necessary ingredients for good hard work that is meaningful and sustainable:

- Motivation
- Sacrifice
- Discipline
- Commitment
- Energy

Motivation

It can be useful to examine your own motivational drives. This summary framework from psychologist Jim Taylor (2012) provides a way to assess what drives you and which factors you may consider leveraging to maintain high levels of effort. Not everyone is impacted by the same elements to the same degree, so honest self-reflection is important to design yourself an effective motivational ecosystem to sustain hard work.

This graphic illustrates two aspects of motivation that are important to understand. First, motivation can be internal or external. Second, it can be positive or negative.

Do you want to avoid punishment, or do you primarily seek rewards? Are you driven by hope or fear? Are you satisfied when you overcome a challenge or reach a goal if no one else knows about it? With this

Internal

• THREATS
• FEAR OF FAILURE
• INADEQUACY
• INSECURITY
• EMBARRASSMENT
Likely outcome: some
change, possible relapse

• CHALLENGE
• DESIRE
• PASSION
• SATISFACTION
• SELF-VALIDATION
Likely outcome: successful
change, fulfillment

Negative   Positive

• FEAR OF JOB LOSS
• LACK OF RESPECT
• SOCIAL PRESSURES
• UNSTABLE LIFE
Likely outcome: some success,
high risk of relapse,
emotional stress

• RECOGNITION
• APPRECIATION
• FINANCIAL REWARDS
• MATERIAL PRIZES
Likely outcome: some change,
partial fulfillment,
dependent on others

External

information, you can begin to design your own accountability system. In general, while the negative aspects above are factors in all our lives, it is generally easy to manage toward the positive. For example, if you are motivated by recognition, then perhaps you submit your best work for an industry annual prize or share achievements with your team and supervisor.

The advantage of being aware of your own motivational drives is that at some point working toward any goal can become tedious and you'll need a reason to push through the rough moments and avoid quitting. As you set up goals and tactical plans, awareness of which levers are most likely to carry you to the finish line helps cultivate perseverance.

Sacrifice

Regardless of the age at which you may have first experienced hard work, success requires sustained levels of effort. There will be days when the outcomes bring joy, and there will be days when the grind becomes tedious, and you will experience the urge to give up. As noted in

Balance (Chapter 3), it is important to recognize when you need a break to recharge, but too many breaks will not get you to your goals. For most people, success requires some degree of personal sacrifice.

Sacrifice means placing the task at hand above your own needs in the moment. It means making a choice to give more to the task than to your own convenience. Being able to sacrifice something that is important to you in order to get something done is a part of hard work at times. It tells people you have a value system, and you value getting the job done more than what your own priorities may dictate in the moment. It tells people about your character, and it will differentiate you as your career grows.

Discipline

Sometimes hard work is about showing up and doing something difficult over time. Like the dairy farmer who doesn't have the luxury of taking a vacation because the cows need milking twice a day, every day. Daily discipline is required to make hard work possible.

> *Motivation will die. Let discipline take its place.*
>
> —Tom Crean
> American Basketball Coach

Discipline says that you *follow a process* of doing that which is required even when facing difficulties. It says that you will stick to the process despite temptations to quit. It says that you have the capacity to get the job done despite whatever comes your way. It says that when you say you will get the job done your word means something. It says when there are a million excuses to quit, the only road you see is the one leading to finish the job.

Commitment

According to David Horsager, a foremost authority on building trust, commitment is one of eight pillars that are necessary to build trust with the others being clarity, compassion, character, competency, connection, contribution, and consistency (Horsager 2011). Commitment means you can be counted on to see things through regardless of what difficulties you face.

When you are committed to a task or job or to another person, you maintain a connection that means something. It means you stand for something. It's important to only commit to things you are serious about and only give your word when you know you can keep it.

Energy

All of the aforementioned elements mean nothing unless you have the energy to see things through. If you don't take care of your body, eat well, rest, and manage your energy level, it doesn't matter how much you want something done if you can't muster the energy to carry the task of the day (see *Well-Being*—Chapter 4).

> *The will to win means nothing if you haven't the will to prepare.*
> —Juma Ikangaa
> 1989 NYC Marathon winner

Make sure you bring the right amount of energy to the task at hand. Have a plan to sustain your level of energy to make sure you can show up to perform your best work. Even if you have the right intentions, a lack of preparation will result in poor performance and maybe even failure on an important part of your life.

Working hard at something you care about can help you achieve more and live a more fulfilling life. While working hard is best judged by your own personal reflection of what you are willing to do to be successful, the five concepts presented earlier should put the odds in your favor.

In summary, make sure you are aware of your own *motivations* in life. Make sure you are willing to *sacrifice* enough to get the job done. When you are pressured to quit or give up, fall back on the process of a personal *disciplined* approach to get you through the tough times. Anchor this process on a steadfast *commitment* to see things through. All the way along the journey, make sure to fuel your body with enough *energy* to stay positive and get the job done.

Shared Wisdom: Lessons From the Road

Experienced professionals credit the willingness to grind when needed as an opportunity to set oneself apart from the competition leading to greater learning and more exciting challenges.

John, a founder and managing partner of a private equity firm, shares his advice on the many benefits of a personal commitment to hard work early in your career.

Use your 20s and early 30s to be a grinder. No one can ever take that work or skillsets or connections you make then away from you. And it will benefit you later in your career.

—John Mickelson, Cofounder and Managing Partner
Midwest Growth Partners, Iowa, USA

A founder and owner of a training and development firm shares the value of hard work and being willing to do things others aren't. Using your time wisely by working harder and smarter than others will pay dividends in the future.

Opportunity is missed by most people because it is dressed in overalls and looks like work. Successful people are usually the ones who are willing to do the things unsuccessful people won't. And many times, that comes down to working hard—and working smart.

Everyone is given the same amount of time in a day; it's how you use that time.

I received this early on from my parents as well as when I sold books door-to-door to pay my way through college.

—Founder and Owner
Training and development company, USA

Rob, a president of a large community college, gives us his "secret of life."

There is a "secret of life," it's hard work.

—Rob Denson, President and CEO
Des Moines Area Community College, Iowa, USA

Rhett, a founder of an engineering consulting firm, shares the value of hard work to achieve meaningful accomplishments in his career.

I wish I had some great insight on how to quickly and efficiently knock down large problems. I don't. The only thing that has worked for me is to focus on the problem and work my tail off to handle it. This usually means working long hours, getting help, and attacking a problem from different angles until a solution is found. I don't have a secret to my success. I've had to work hard to achieve everything that I've been able to accomplish that is meaningful in my career.

—Rhett Schildroth, Founder
RedShield Consulting, Iowa, USA

Chad, an engineering manager, shares the power of hard work and focusing on doing a job well and how this will lead to career opportunities.

Do a good job and work hard in your current position and that will open the door for future opportunities.

—Chad Grainger, Engineering Manager
John Deere, Iowa, USA

Craig, a president of an IT consulting firm, shares his advice on how to become the best by doing things most people aren't willing to do.

If you want to be one of the best, you must be willing to do what most people won't do. It is a message that I continually pass on to my staff and my teenage sons. I use this advice in work and wellness.

—Craig Jackman, President
Paragon IT Professionals, Iowa, USA

Brian, a founder and president of a consulting firm after having a successful career in the insurance industry, shares advice he received from his father about always treating your job as if you were an owner, and how much it has influenced his career.

My father was a CEO of a Fortune 500 company. I asked him early in my own career what was the most important factor in his own success. He told me no matter what job he had with the company he treated that job as if he owned the company. This was great advice because of its simplicity, take ownership in every job that you do no matter how large the task.

—Bryan Neary, President
CSG Actuarial Consulting, Nebraska, USA

Reflections: What's Your Story?

1. What are your main insights/takeaways from the chapter at this moment?

_____

_____

_____

_____

_____

_____

_____

_____

_____

2. What are one to three goals/intentions you would like to set for yourself?

_____

_____

_____

_____

_____

_____

_____

_____

_____

Going Further: Questions, Readings, and References

Discussion Questions

11.1 Tony talks about his work ethic and how it was formed over the years. What is your work ethic and how would you explain it to someone?

11.2 Having a strong work ethic will help you achieve more in life, but it will also lead to other benefits. What parts of your life would benefit by having a strong work ethic?

11.3 Think about a time when you had to sacrifice something important to you to achieve a goal. Was it worth it? Why or why not?

11.4 Where do you lie on the motivational matrix? How can you leverage this to ensure you continue to work hard over time?

11.5 When was the first time you worked for someone else and got paid for it? Has this influenced how you carry yourself today? How might this benefit your professional career?

Suggested Reading

Allen, D. 2001. *Getting Things Done*. New York, NY: Viking Penguin.

Godin, S. 2010. *Linchpin: Are You Indispensable? How to Drive Your Career and Create a Remarkable Future*. Hachette UK.

Horsager, D.B. 2021. *Trusted Leader: 8 Pillars That Drive Results*. Oakland, CA: Berrett Koedler.

Olson, J. 2013. *The Slight Edge: Turning Simple Disciplines into Massive Success and Happiness*. 8th Anniversary ed. Austin, TX: Greenleaf Book Group Press.

Pink, D. 2009. *Drive: The Surprising Truth About What Motivates Us*. New York, NY: Riverhead Books.

Sterner, T. 2012. *The Practicing Mind: Developing Focus and Discipline in Your Life Master Any Skill or Challenge by Learning to Love the Process*. Novato, CA: New World Library.

References

Horsager, D.B. 2011. *The Trust Edge*. New York, NY: Free Press.

Taylor, J. January 02, 2012. "Personal Growth Motivation: The Drive to Change." *Psychology Today*.

CHAPTER 12

Relationships

RELATIONSHIPS
AUTHENTICITY
EMPATHY
DIVERSITY
BE PRESENT
BE PREPARED

The currency of real networking is not greed but generosity.

—Keith Ferrazzi
American Author

Introduction

All of us are the sum total of the experiences we have lived up to this moment. Those experiences have made us who we are today and will continue to create who we become in the future. Every day of our life we make a contribution to our future self by all we come across in our daily routine.

One of the most important ingredients of who we become is the relationships that we have and the quality and depth of our network with others.

Building strong relationships throughout your lifetime is like being a tree that produces fruit every day all year long. You grow and learn by your interactions with others. Instead of relying only on your experience, you can tap into the experience of many others. You gain by having a second set of eyes on a particular issue. You enlist a "second brain" to help you think through a difficult issue.

The benefits of building strong relationships are never-ending for you as well as your contribution to others. Taking the time to invest in relationships will always be time well spent.

Tony's Lessons From Personal Experience

The first phone call I received in my professional career was from another employee named Roger Bernard to join his summer softball team in Waterloo. I didn't know it at the time, but this one call eventually helped me learn more about our company, learn faster, have more fun, and eventually led me to new opportunities in the company.

I was hired by John Deere as a chemical engineer and worked on the shop floor where we made parts for John Deere tractors. There were five other John Deere businesses operating in the area: a global engineering center, a foundry, an engine factory, a hydraulic pump business, and an assembly plant. There were people from all units who played on Roger's softball team, and I met people from other teams during that first summer I worked for Deere. A couple of them previously worked in the field with our dealer organization, which was my long-term career interest at that point in my career.

One conversation led to another over a couple of years. During this time, I was careful to stay focused on doing the best I could possibly do in my current job. Then came a few recommendations to talk to a few more people and eventually an opportunity came my way to join the Kansas City Sales Branch. This dramatically changed my view of the company as I worked with dealers and customers and to this day remains some of the most impactful experiences I have ever had in my career.

Throughout my life, networking has always led to personal and professional growth. I view it as a form of engagement, a way to lean into life, to take action, and to learn new things. In some ways, I view the benefits of networking as winning in many ways: learning and growth, new friends, and just maybe you'll be given the opportunity to help someone else along in their journey.

Each of us brings a special talent to this world and the world wouldn't be the same without what we contribute. However, our highest contribution to this world doesn't occur in a vacuum. There is a harmony of relationships at play in real time in everything we do every day of our life. We stand upon the shoulders of human civilization together with those who came before us. We also stand in the moment with those who stand next to us. Each one of us is absolutely unique, but we also live in a world/community that is dependent upon relationships if we hope to achieve our highest common good on this earth.

Building your circle of contacts can certainly benefit your career and lead to a more fulfilling life. But like building long-term relationships, it can also help you live a more fulfilling life. It may come at you in small ways like that phone call from Roger on my first day at work, or it may come from more structured interactions like school activities for children or events at work designed to get people to know each other a little better.

Building a personal and professional network should be on everyone's list as they think about what it takes to have a successful career and a more fulfilling life.

Leading Practices

The leading practices below are broken into two categories: Relationships and Networking. The first four leading practices below help you create and sustain high-quality *relationships* in your professional and social circles. The next five leading practices address the critical importance of *networking* to increase the breadth and depth of your relationships.

Relationships

As humans who live in community with one another, developing and nurturing relationships is a natural part of our being. We are hard-wired to be social creatures. But that doesn't mean it comes easily to everyone.

- Be You: Be Authentic
- The Platinum Rule: Practice Empathy
- Celebrate Diversity
- Be Where Your Feet Are: Be Present

Be You: Be Authentic

In order to be a good friend or colleague, you need to bring and share your most authentic self. Just like managing multiple social media accounts, it can be nearly impossible to manage different personas for different groups of people. Therefore, one of the first and most important rules of creating and sustaining strong relationships is to *be authentic*. For some of us, this may be difficult. We may not know who we are with confidence, but even honestly representing a journey of self-discovery with someone else can provide a solid foundation for a mutually beneficial friendship. Along with authenticity comes the recommendation to *be vulnerable*. Paradoxically, vulnerability yields confidence and power. It is very difficult to be authentic without being vulnerable. By sharing your quirky fascination with turtles or Willy Wonka doesn't make you a weirdo. It makes you human and interesting and endearing and memorable to those around you. Your authentic self deserves to be in relationships; your friends and colleagues deserve to know.

The Platinum Rule: Relate With Empathy

We often hear the golden rule referenced as one of the most universally shared human values. However, we have found the platinum rule can be even more powerful to remind us about the importance of other-oriented empathy. The *golden rule* suggests we should treat others in the same way that you would like to be treated. The *platinum rule*, by contrast, recommends that we should treat others the way they themselves would like to be treated. This slight difference can make a big difference in creating and maintaining relationships. By turning the focus outward to the preferences of those around us, we can stay actively curious and engaged with the needs and emotions of others.

Celebrate Diversity

The two maxims of *the Platinum Rule* and *Be You: Be Authentic* also require that you authentically accept and celebrate the diversity of others. By celebrating their differences, you honor others' authentic selves. This diversity can be represented across a multitude of dimensions-of-difference: gender, national heritage, race, ethnicity, linguistic traditions, religious beliefs, sexual orientation, functional specialties, political viewpoints, and the list could go on and on. At present, polarization and division among people along these lines of identity is all too common. It can be difficult to even be in the same room with someone who doesn't hold your same beliefs. However, it can also be incredibly rewarding to engage in relationship with others who are different than you. You may just learn something if you listen and remain open-minded. After all, life would be pretty boring if we only surrounded ourselves with people just like ourselves.

Be Where Your Feet Are: Be Present and Show Up

Being present means you are invested in relationships no matter how big or small. When you are with a friend or team member, be where your feet are. While that conversation or question may not be the most important thing on your to-do list, it may be the most important gift you can give to someone else in that particular moment. And those moments matter.

Networking

The next five leading practices address the specific goal of networking to increase your breadth of relationships. Many leaders have a love–hate relationship with networking. Some love it while others avoid it like the plague. However, as one author put it, "*If networking makes you feel dirty, you're doing it wrong*" (Clark 2021). Here are some leading practices that can help you build a fruitful and rewarding network:

- It's Not All About You: Get Over It!
- Be Prepared: Know Your Script
- Commit to It
- Follow-Through and Follow-Up!
- Pay It Forward

It's Not All About You: Get Over It!

One of the biggest misconceptions about networking is that it is self-indulgent and self-serving. However, reframing this perspective is key to developing successful networking skills and mutually beneficial relationships.

Before the pandemic, we would always recommend visualizing walking to a room with a hand outstretched (#HandshakePose). This could be interpreted literally or metaphorically, but the point is this: Be welcoming to others and they are much more likely to be gracious and welcoming in return. At the beginning, networking can sometimes seem awkward. However, if you realize that it's not all about you, and get over the expectation that you have to wow/dazzle everyone you meet with your wit and charm, you will survive long enough to get some good networking practice that will increase your comfort and confidence over time. Remember, networking can be as easy as inviting someone to play in a softball game!

Be Prepared: Know Your Script

Now, once you've left all that awkwardness and self-doubt behind, you've got to be prepared. Even the most confident networkers have a few go-to questions/phrases they use to strike up a conversation. Here are some great examples of icebreakers to get things going:

- Know your introduction.
  - It may change depending on the event/circumstance, but it should align to your interests/goals for meeting that person at that event. Here's a very simple example: *Hello, my name is Carter and I'm here to build my network.*
- After your introduction, you can ask loads of different types of questions. A good Google search for "*sample networking conversation questions*" will provide you with a lifetime of engaging queries (Go Networking 2022). Here are a few of our favorites:
  - I'm very curious about your journey. Tell me how you came to your role as _____ at _____ organization.
  - What do you love to do? Or what are you most passionate about these days? What gets you out of bed in the morning?
  - What are some of the most significant changes you've seen in your organization over the past _____ years? In your industry? In yourself?

- So, what's next? What are your goals for the next _____ months or years?
- Now, once you've broken the ice with your charming wit and had a great conversation with your new best friends, you're going to want to refreeze the ice to make sure no one else swoops in and takes advantage of the friendly atmosphere. So, right before you walk away, you should thank them for their time then refreeze the ice by dropping this little cheerful nugget: *Death comes to us all... goodbye!* If anyone comes after you, they won't stand a chance (Acaster 2021)!

Commit to It

Once you have mastered the art of the networking conversation, it's time to take it to the next level. What are some specific targets that will inspire you and help you achieve your goals? Here are some good examples:

- If growing your network is a priority, we've seen many leaders set a target to meet 100 new people a year. Be sure to track your progress and don't forget to follow up with your new friends. So they don't feel like they were only a pebble on your path to achieving your goal.
- If deepening your network is a priority, consider how you may push beyond normal conversations to increase trust, confidence, and psychological safety. Sometimes this means sharing a meal together. Or going on a trip together. These shared experiences serve to deepen relationships.
- Finally, memberships in professional and/or social organizations are great ways to expand and deepen your network. It may involve volunteering, or serving on a board, or simply joining an organization to learn more functional knowledge and meet new people. Be a joiner, contribute meaningfully, and we guarantee you will receive more than you could ever hope to give.

Follow-Through and Follow-Up!

It goes without saying, but once you have met someone new in your network. You must follow through on any commitments you've made to that person. That may be as simple as following up with him/her on LinkedIn or social media, or it could be following through on your promise to help them find Chicago Bears football tickets! No matter what it is, be sure to follow through and follow up occasionally to keep the relationship healthy.

Pay It Forward

As a final note, please remember that to whom much has been given much is expected. If you have received an introduction from a friend, then you could pay-it-forward by introducing others where appropriate. Don't only make withdrawals from your network, but deposit social capital back so that you become known as someone that gives back to your community.

Your networks form the fabric of your life. For example, in *Self-Image* (Chapter 1), we learned that we find identity through our associations with our employer, professional societies, family and friends, clubs, spiritual communities, sports, and so on. How you relate to others in this world really does matter. As you think about your relationships, and the people who mean the most in your life, reflect on how they started and developed over time. Did it just happen like in a family, or did you invest in them over time? Chances are, some you may have grown up with and some you created along the way.

Shared Wisdom: Lessons From the Road

Relationships color our personal and professional lives and represent a powerful opportunity for us to not only get the most out of life but also to enjoy the journey.

Jarret, a successful sales executive turned founder of his own firm, shares the importance of relationships over the long term and how important it is to cultivate strong relationships at every stage of your career.

I am not sure that I can make that call specifically. What I have done to this point has become the fabric of who I am. To state that I would have taken any part of what I have accomplished away would mean that that experience lost would have changed my outlook at every level of personal/professional growth. From working in a warehouse to fill orders, inside sales associate, outside sales, US Sales and Marketing VP for a small manufacturer and now a principal owner in a sales and marketing company, I have always held fast to the experience and how it was the right place for me at the right time and that is precious to me. If I could have changed anything, it would have been to hold on to more of the close relationships that I have developed and nurtured them to a higher degree. I feel that in the haste of everyday work life, too much of the close relationships I have had throughout my life got lost in the fold. I would always look back and hope that those would rekindle themselves at some point when the time was right, but in hindsight I would say that the ability to stay/get really close again have been lost in the fabric of time. I will still take the opportunity to make them better but a whole generation of life has come and gone for most of them and that is lost opportunity to be part of a tighter bond amongst once really good friends.

—Jarret Golwitzer, Cofounder and President
Integrated Sales Inc., Iowa, USA

Susan, author and president of a consulting firm, shares how a network of trusted advisors sustained her in challenging moments of her career.

I've had many—how to tackle reporting unethical behavior (I feared the reporting could be career ending for me); balancing work/life and childcare choices; lulls in consulting work that made me question my choice to be solo. All of them solved by talking it through with people I knew and trusted and who knew and trusted me. Your network sustains you in so many ways.

—Susan (Finerty) Zelmanski, President
Finerty Consulting, Illinois, USA

Kelly, a mental health counselor, shares her realization midcareer that she needed a broader network to take her career to the next level.

I would have focused on developing cross-functional relationships earlier in my career. For many years I let my work speak for itself and was greatly rewarded with promotions and moves. While I was enjoying the upward movement, it wasn't until I was in my 40s that I decided to really dig in and assess what I was passionate about and what I wanted to be when I grew up. I then began voicing my desire to change the direction of my career path; however, I did not have a network established and it was impossible to do within the same company.

—Kelly Kreiter Penning
Mental Health Counselor at Family Resources
and Executive Director of New Kingdom Trailriders
Iowa, USA

David, a retired executive, shares his simple and direct advice to network and develop relationships that lead to trust, which ultimately drives change.

Network, develop relationships, embrace change. Nothing happens until trust is established midcareer.

—David Delagardelle, Retired Executive
John Deere, Iowa, USA

Bob, a sales manager, shares how he took on extra responsibilities to gain experience outside his current role and how this led to greater professional and personal growth.

Six Sigma allowed me to lead project teams and improve processes through change. That allows me to work with people that I do not get to work with in my normal role. The Teleworkers Unlimited employee resource group also broadens my network and opens more minds to nontraditional work environments. Neither has been easy or resolved my problem of achieving my goal of a promotion and lead-

ing a team but both make me better as a professional and personally, which defines success to me even without winning that much sought-after promotion. I know I am still growing and genuinely understand empathy better than when I was younger.

—Bob Petrosino, Territory Sales Manager
John Deere, New Jersey, USA

Roland, a sales director, shares his advice on building a strong network and the impact it could have when faced with challenging career issues.

Looking back I probably should have kept my eyes more open and established a larger network outside of my previous company, given that my unit was shut down.

—Roland Forster, Sales Director
Kersia, Zurich, Switzerland

Mike, a president and owner of a recruiting firm, shares the value of getting networked with a recruiter earlier in his career.

Now that I am a recruiter I see the value of having one in your network. Knowing my companies had issues, I wish I would have connected with a recruiter sooner, been more open to opportunities when they presented themselves, and I wish I would have been more proactive driving my career. Not sure loyalty is rewarded as much anymore.

—Mike McNulty, President and Owner
Synergy Recruiting Solutions, Des Moines, IA, USA

Reflections: What's Your Story?

1. What are your main insights/takeaways from the chapter at this moment?

_____

_____

_____

_____

_____

_____

_____

_____

_____

_____

2. What are one to three goals/intentions you would like to set for yourself?

_____

_____

_____

_____

_____

_____

_____

_____

_____

_____

_____

_____

Going Further: Questions, Readings, and References

Discussion Questions

12.1 How can the quality of your network expand in the next 12 months? Wider? Deeper? Professional Memberships?

12.2 If the goal of networking comes from a place of generosity, what do you have to give the world that would make it a better place to live? Make a list in the margins of this book.

12.3 What are the strongest relationships you have in your network today? What about them makes it so?

12.4 In the margins of this book, jot down the most impactful people of your life. Think about why they are so impactful. If someone else would do this same exercise, how can you be recognized in the "margin of their book"?

12.5 Pick out a conversation with someone you know well in the next day and focus on listening. Don't worry about how you will respond. Just listen and focus on really understanding what they are saying. Before you respond in any way, take note of what that felt like. How can you develop better relationships through better listening skills?

Suggested Reading

Carnegie, D. 1964. *How to Win Friends and Influence People*. New York, NY: Simon and Schuster.

Ferrazzi, K., and T. Raz. 2014. *Never Eat Alone, Expanded and Updated: And Other Secrets to Success, One Relationship at a Time*. New York, NY: Crown Business.

Gerber, S., and R. Paugh. 2018. *Super Connector: Stop Networking and Start Building Business Relationships That Matter*. New York, NY: De Capo Press.

Peters, W. 2019. *An Integrated Life of Leadership*. 918 Studio Press.

References

Clark, D. 2021. "If Networking Makes You Feel Dirty, You're Doing It Wrong." *The New York Times*. www.wsj.com/articles/if-networking-makes-you-feel-dirty-youre-doing-it-wrong-11631883600

Go Networking. n.d. "15 Questions for Your Business Networking Success." https://gonetworking.com.au/15-questions-business-networking-success/

www.jamesacaster.com

CHAPTER 13

Adversity

ADVERSITY
POSITIVITY
FAILURE
INTENTION
FOCUS

Failure is not the opposite of success. Failure is part of success.

—William Ritter

Author

Introduction

Adversity and tough times visit us all sooner or later. Something unexpected will rear its ugly head, something in the environment will change that you hadn't considered, or your own personal circumstances may change in ways you hadn't imagined. There are some certainties in life, such as death and taxes, but change will always occur. The longer you live you will face tough times.

The only question it seems worth studying is how will you react when the tough times come along?

The difference between success and failure is sometimes a very fine line. When do you succumb to tough times and when do you persevere? How committed are you to getting the job done despite how arduous the journey has become? Each situation presents an opportunity to reinforce your commitment to learning, growth, and hard work. Knowing that each is a learning situation is great self-awareness, and taking the time to harvest this learning during difficult times will earn you wisdom beyond your years.

Tony's Lessons From Personal Experience

Earlier in my life, I had an attitude about failing and it was not a very positive one. It was kind of simple and naïve. Basically, failing sucked. It wasn't just that I failed at something, but it was the indictment that came with it. Failing never seemed like an event. It seemed more like a part of me that never went away. It hung over my head like a halo to remind me that while I had failed at something once in my life, *it can always happen again.* I reacted to failure by extending it as part of my character and by doing so it controlled my attitude about everything.

Probably the worst part of it all was that not only did I fail, but *I was a failure.* If Thomas Edison had that kind of relationship with failure we'd all still be in the dark.

But what about the times went things went right? Was the opposite true? Did success represent an indictment of my character? Did achievement hang over my head like a halo? Did I extend that feeling of accomplishment like an organ of my body? Did it control my attitude? When I did something that turned out successful, was I a success?

For a moment, it feels awesome when things fall my way. But more often than not, success fades faster than the hangover from failing. Failing had a bigger tail than success did, and I tended to internalize the causes of failure to my character while assigning success as the outcome of luck, being in the right place at the right time, or coming from the efforts of others.

Failure was simply on me, but success, however, was an outcome of more complex factors.

Early in my career, I was assigned to fix a serious problem we had in manufacturing that involved brake parts. We bonded brake pads to large steel plates and the pads were falling off in transit to dealers' parts departments. I designed new fixtures for the assembly in the bonding process, experimented with different adhesives, tried different brake pad materials, tested different temperatures to cure the adhesives, and even developed elaborate nondestructive testing after the assembly to ensure no bad parts were sent to the line. It was incredibly complex and frustrating as nothing seemed to work. Through trial and error over six months, working with union members, engineers, suppliers, and University of Northern Iowa professors, we eventually found a solution that dramatically improved the process.

It was hard for me to deal with the constant testing and failing for months on end. I took it personally and labeled myself a failure. I lost sleep, brought my problems home, and let it darken my mood on weekends. What did I ultimately learn? Teamwork, ingenuity, experimental design, tool and die design, and many other skills. I also learned that ultimately some problems in life are just not easy to solve. Some problems take more time. I also learned confidence. I learned persistence. I learned diligence. I learned how to carry failure as a temporary milestone as part of my journey to success. I learned each failed experiment was a step closer to the end.

I also learned it is OK to fail and maybe even feel like a failure, *as long as you keep moving forward and taking the next step.*

You have choices to make when it comes to reacting to the world around you. The famous formula E+R=O stands for Event + Reaction = Outcome (Canfield and Switzer 2015). Any event has no meaning by itself. Only when we attach our Reaction, and only then, can we truly predict the Outcome. In every event in our life, we hold the power to choose our reaction. Choosing to be positive and constructive is way better than allowing negativity to bore into the marrow of your bones and dominate your life. A key to success is recognizing that it is indeed "a choice" we have to make.

Building a strong, positive relationship with adversity is part of being successful. Finding the positive in both success and failure is a key to your growth. Learning this early in your career will help you in many ways to build a successful career and a more fulfilling life.

Leading Practices

Misfortune and tough times will be a part of everyone's life at some point or another. How you react to it will mean all the difference in the world quite literally. Using adversity as a means of growth will lead to a constructive relationship with failure, resilience in building a positive attitude, and diligence in staying on task no matter what comes your way.

Positivity

Knowing how our minds and bodies work can help us maintain a positive attitude—even in the face of adversity. Five concepts listed below can help maintain a healthy and positive perspective through all life's ups and downs:

- Recognize That Failure Lasts Longer
- Develop Positivity as a Critical Leadership Trait
- Reject Failure's Three Ps: Pervasive, Permanent, and Personal
- Counting Contributions
- Practice Positive Visualization

Recognize That Failure Lasts Longer

According to Dr. Roy Baumeister and his coauthors, the fundamental notion of "good" and "bad" is one of the first and most important concepts we learn as a child. Furthermore, they assert that "bad is stronger than good" throughout so many aspects of life (Baumeister, Bratslavsky, Finkenauer, and Vohs 2021). So what does this practically mean for us as humans, workers, and leaders? Well, for starters, it explains why Tony might dwell upon his failures more intensely than he would internalize his successes. It also explains why we are not incredibly reckless when pursuing big goals. After all, it is indeed better to stay alive than to die trying. The evolutionary basis makes sense: if you focus on avoiding bad outcomes, you stand a better chance of surviving long enough to pass along your genes (Tugend 2012).

Thankfully most of us aren't worried about survival every day. So, when we focus too strongly/frequently on negativity—either within ourselves or in the world around us—we need to pause and ask: *Is that an accurate assessment of the situation?* Or is it simply a product of our natural genetic and psychological predispositions? This brief pause gives us the opportunity to *self-assess with intention.* Or we can ask other trusted friends/colleagues for their own opinion/assessment (because we know enough to question our natural tendencies)! By the way, getting into the habit of asking a trusted person in your life for their opinion is a great way to build self-awareness.

Develop Positivity as a Critical Leadership Trait

Harvard Business Review recognized positivity as one of the most transformational leadership ideas over the last 20 years (Fryer 2004). In general, if you aspire to leadership, you must be positive. What would motivate people to follow someone who is consistently negative? It just doesn't happen (Russell 2021)!

Whereas Sigmund Freud starts with the assumption that humans are caustic and conflicted creatures, Maslow and others successfully challenged that assumption to emphasize the inherent goodness of humans (Caza and Cameron 2008). This core assumption supports the subsequent development of positivity as a core leadership trait across time and cultures. Not only is positivity consistently recognized as central to effective leadership, but we also know that positive teams are more productive (Seppala 2015). While we cannot cover all the practical tips for how to develop your own positive leadership framework, Kim Cameron's book *Positive Leadership* provides a tremendous introduction and how-to guide (Cameron 2012).

Rejecting Failure's Three Ps

It is best to develop a conscious relationship with how you view failure early in your career. The American psychologist, Martin Seligman, believes our innate reactions to failure can be pervasive, permanent, and personal (see figure below). In order to develop and sustain a positive approach, we must fundamentally reject the three Ps of failure—recognizing Zig Ziglar's reminder that: "Failure is an event, not a person" (Seligman 2006).

Pessimistic	Optimistic
Permanent	Temporary
Pervasive	Specific
Personal	External

Counting Contributions

In their 2017 book *Option B*, Sheryl Sandberg and Adam Grant suggest a practice of counting contributions (Sandberg and Grant 2017). They suggest that "counting blessings" doesn't necessarily inspire sustainable future positive action. However, counting and writing down three contributions they made each day builds confidence and momentum. Contributions are fundamentally active choices. By regularly writing down past positive contributions, it becomes easier to recognize and repeat those contributions in the future.

Practice Positive Visualization

Sometimes, our minds can be scary places filled with horrifying images of metaphorical monsters of what could potentially happen in an imagined future. By envisioning all the different ways that a situation can go horribly wrong, we can become paralyzed. This is called catastrophizing. However, the opposite is also true if we focus on the positive. Positive visualization can be an important practice to develop and maintain. In Buddhism, it is said that "all that we are is the result of what we have thought. The mind is everything. What we think we become." (Hoque 2017). Instead of creating mental monsters, it can be incredibly liberating to imagine all the positive possible outcomes of a particular situation. Now, we know this is difficult because we learned previously that bad is stronger than good.

However, with practice, visualizing your future goals and even how you may feel after achieving those goals is a profoundly powerful mindset shift. Furthermore, you are infinitely more likely to achieve those goals if you can visualize them in vivid detail.

Diligence

If we follow the definition of diligence as careful and persistent effort, then it is possible to cultivate these tendencies in yourself. If you feel like you need to work on improving your diligence, the items listed below are a great place to start:

- *Time*: It is our most valuable resource. Many successful people have very robust time management skills in which they allocate blocks of time for their highest and best use. The key issue here is are you investing your time in your highest priorities? Use the calendar test to hold yourself accountable—review how you used the last 90 days and did you focus your time on your highest priorities?
- *Intention*: Being proactive in deciding how to expend effort and making sure that these choices align with an envisioned destination. While everyone hopes that the right opportunities will come along, working with intention means you're not waiting but rather actively creating the openings you want. When and how do you think about the days, weeks, and months ahead? Making being intentional a habit will lead to a more positive life.
- *Organization*: In a busy world, people may feel overwhelmed by the number of tasks they need to accomplish, information overload, and uncertainty around them. Getting a system in place to sort through the noise helps mitigate the pace of modern life. One great system is a simple mind map where you write down everything in your mind on a sheet of paper. Getting everything from your mind committed to paper will be a very powerful first step in tackling the most important issues more productively.

- *Focus*: Since the publication of *Deep Work* (Newport 2016), there has been increased scrutiny of the idea that endless multitasking is the key to success. This approach encourages us to devote focused time to work without distraction for the most important outcomes we want to reach. According to the late Stanford professor Clifford Nass, an expert in human and technology interfaces, it is technically impossible to multitask. Coming to terms with this reality and finding time to truly focus on what is important will help you lead a better life.

Summary

Chances are you will face more than a few difficult challenges in your life. Some may be personal, and some may be professional. Some may seem obvious and urgent, while others may creep up on you over time.

It's important to have a positive relationship with challenges because it's in the tough spots where you learn the most. It's in the tough spots when you find out what you are made of. It's in the tough spots where you separate yourself from the rest. It's in the tough spots where you make decisions that ultimately lead to the opportunity for leadership. Long before you should lead others, you should learn to lead yourself. Especially during the tough times.

Not only are challenges, diligence, and positivity the nature of work and progress, they are *also the nature of growth.*

Shared Wisdom: Lessons From the Road

The relationship between adversity and growth can be very personal and sometimes painful. Whether addressing discrimination in the workplace or dealing with internal conflict about the future of your life, a tremendous amount of good can come to your life by facing adversity constructively.

When we asked our community of leaders to share their stories, they boldly shared their experiences—and advice—for our benefit.

Leonardo, a director of technology, shares his approach to breaking down major challenges into key areas of focus eventually leading to small tasks and daily priorities.

The biggest problem I ever faced was to keep the focus. To resolve it, I have been working on many strategies in the last years. First, it is to define main goals, even for small tasks. Then I divide the goals into activities and then I try to sort the activities through my calendar, reserving some time for a coffee and relax.

—Leonardo Chechi, Director of Technology
Cruzeiro do Sul Grãos Ltda,
Ribeirão Preto, Brazil

Ana, an analyst from Mexico, shares some great advice about how to view challenges, and how she turned a difficult situation into a learning experience.

My professional career began four years ago, and I received the best advice I could ever get just a year after it began. Just as I was starting to work in a new position, my supervisor said to me something along the lines of: "Always be glad of new challenges because the day there are none, that's the day where you've settled in your comfort zone."

One time I changed positions, and the person who was going to deliver their activities to me was not cooperating and was not happy to teach me how to do their job. I had to learn every task practically by myself with little to no knowledge of the process. Although it was a problem in my career, I managed to turn it into something positive because my learning curve developed sooner.

—Ana Victoria Garza, Operations Analyst
John Deere, Mexico

Kiley, a president and CEO of a nonprofit, shares his advice to lean into the tough work earlier in his life and career.

I would have worked harder as an elementary student, which would have taught me to work harder in high school, which would have led to better performance in college, which would have set me on a course toward greater career success. We may remember the monu-

mental decisions, but it's the incremental, everyday decisions that matter most.

—Kiley Miller, President and CEO
Trees Forever, Iowa, USA

Morgan, a digital product manager, shares a deeply personal story about the challenges she faced and how her positive reaction in the moment led to substantial opportunities down the road.

I once worked for a manager who clearly treated me unfairly compared to my male peer. It was the most demotivating time of my career. I felt disrespected, underutilized, and worthless. I decided to define my own worth instead of letting others define my value. I put in extra effort to enable my own opportunities by reading, learning, researching, and networking. I worked closely with my male colleague (who treated me very fairly) to seek a deeper understanding and responsibility from him. He was very willing and supportive and taught me the technical learning I was otherwise deprived of by the situation. I intentionally focused my energy on a positive attitude each day. I executed small habits to reflect such as listing five things that I did well every day or grade myself on how well I demonstrated positivity each day. Eventually, I was offered a new opportunity under a new manager that launched me into a series of very wonderful job opportunities.

I continue to reflect on this experience throughout my career to remind myself how to overcome situations I can't completely control.

—Morgan Halverson, Digital Product Manager
John Deere Financial, Iowa, USA

Richard, president of a personal financial services firm, shares how the decisions made early in his career when faced with adversity opened up a powerful combination of discipline and purpose that channeled his future success.

The biggest problem I faced was finding my initial direction. I always had ability but did not initially have discipline. After dropping out of college after less than a year I chose to join the Army. That turned out to be the single, smartest decision I have made in my life. The Army instilled the discipline that allowed me to develop and channel my abilities.

—Richard C. Salmen, President
Family Investment Center, Kansas, USA

A business school dean of a major university shares a deeply personal story about her father and what his experience meant for her career and the values she carries with her to this day.

Good leaders live their values and sometimes that means you lose your job. I learned this while I was in college from my father as he explained to me the situation that led to his losing his job. As the highest-level manager at a location in Mississippi during the 1980s, he was unhappy with the discrimination he saw in pay for African Americans, all men, who worked for the firm. Over several years, he increased the wages for these men based on their productivity relative to other men in similar positions. Same productivity, same wages. This was not supported by his supervisor located at headquarters out of state and thus his pink slip. By watching him, I also learned that there is never ANY job that is beneath you. If getting something done means you jump in the ditch, shovel in hand, and help the team get something done, you do it. I can only hope that I live these values as he did.

—Business School Dean
Higher education, USA

Jay, a senior executive in the agriculture industry, shares the power of using personal failures to build greater knowledge and help others on their journey as well.

While certain decisions rendered by me resulted in failure, each failure led to greater knowledge that has aided myself in helping others to avoid similar failures while encouraging others to avoid the fear of failure.

—Jay Pickrel, VP, Aftermarket
Gooseneck Equipment, North Dakota, USA

Ricardo, a senior executive in the financial services industry, shares advice he received from his uncle on how to manage any challenges life may throw at you.

> *Early in my career, I got advice from one of my uncles; he told me life is simple, you just have to work hard, have passion in anything you do, treat people (everyone) the way you would like to be treated, and always do the right thing no matter how difficult it is to do it.*
> —Ricardo Leal, VP International Finance (Retired)
> John Deere Financial, São Paulo, Brazil

Ralf, a university professor, shares the observation that life in general is a challenging experience and the power of always "looking ahead" versus getting stuck in the past.

> *Life's road is bumpy. Learning from the past and growing from experience is extremely important. I would recommend using the lessons learned to look ahead instead of ruminating about the past.*
> —Ralf Lanwehr, Professor of International Management
> University of Applied Sciences Sudwestfalen, Germany

Jenny, a retired senior executive, shares a personal regret as she reflects on missed opportunities to advocate more for herself and address improper behavior more directly in the moment.

> *I wish I would have felt comfortable advocating for myself as a woman. I was harassed twice. Both times I made low-level jokey comments to leaders, like "Hey—don't seat me next to xyz at the next team dinner—he had a little too much to drink and thought we were on a date!" I made it sound funny, so I made it easy to ignore.*
> —Jenny Kimball, Retired Executive
> South Carolina, USA

Rocky, a senior technical leader with experience in major Fortune 100 companies as well as several startups, shares his experience in navigating challenging career issues when discerning your true passion.

Four years into my first job after college at a large company, I nervously asked an Agile coach for career advice. Should I stay in my comfortable position or quit for a risky startup in an unfamiliar industry? He admitted he couldn't make the decision for me, but correctly guessed I'd already made up my mind and was too scared to admit it to myself. It was the final push I needed to join the startup and learn faster than I thought possible.

—Rocky Warren, Principal Architect, Tech Lead, and Product Manager
Vertex Software, Colorado, USA

Carrie, founder and CEO of a sustainability startup, shares her experience in dealing with organizational change and the need to consider moving on earlier if the right support isn't found in new leadership.

When I found myself twice reorganized with new leaders who made it clear they didn't value me or my style, I stuck it out thinking I will show how fabulous and valuable I am. Especially as I was in a work area I was passionate about. I also thought they might move on; however, they didn't. I should have moved earlier as it's soul destroying to be undervalued and even sadly disrespected.

—Carrie Lomas, Founder
Brand Conscious, London, England

Reflections: What's Your Story?

1. What are your main insights/takeaways from the chapter at this moment?

_____

_____

_____

_____

_____

_____

_____

_____

_____

2. What are one to three goals/intentions you would like to set for yourself?

_____

_____

_____

_____

_____

_____

_____

_____

_____

Going Further: Questions, Readings, and References

Discussion Questions

13.1   Tony talked about his reaction to failure and how it dominated his attitude at times. Think about your own experiences with failure for a moment. How did you personally process the experiences and what can you learn from them?

13.2   Many leaders look back at challenges they faced in their life and acknowledge the growth they gained through the struggles they faced. How can you anticipate these struggles and prepare yourself to thrive through adversity?

13.3   Matthew and Jeffrey point out Martin Seligman's 3 Ps of failure—pervasive, permanent, and personal. Think back to a time when you failed and reflect on the three Ps. How could you have reacted differently?

13.4   During times of adversity, it can help to stay diligent and not get distracted by the struggles of the day. Think back to a time when you were challenged—how did you manage your time, intentionality, organization, and focus?

13.5   List 10 things in the margins of this book that you can do to be a more positive person, then write on your calendar 90 days from now to come back and check this page. Did you make it happen?

Suggested Reading

Dweck, C. 2016. *Mindset: The New Psychology of Success.* New York, NY: Ballantine Books.

Harford, T. 2011. *Adapt: Why Success Always Starts With Failure.* New York, NY: Farrar, Straus, and Giroux.

McCall, Lombardo, and Morrison.1988. *The Lessons of Experience.* New York, NY: Lexington Books.

Sandberg, S., and A. Grant. 2017. *Option B: Facing Adversity, Building Resilience, and Finding Joy.* New York, NY: Alfred A. Knopf.

References

Baumeister, R.F., E. Bratslavsky, C. Finkenauer, and K.D. Vohs. 2001. "Bad Is Stronger Than Good." *Review of General Psychology* 5, no. 4, pp. 323–370.

Cameron, K. 2012. *Positive Leadership: Strategies for Extraordinary Performance.* Berrett-Koehler Publishers.

Canfield, J. and J. Switzer. 2015. *The Success Principles: How to Get From Where You Are to Where You Want to Be.* Boston, MA: Mariner Books.

Caza, A., and K.S. Cameron. 2008. "Positive Organizational Scholarship: What Does It Achieve." *Handbook of macro-organizational behavior,* pp. 99–116.

Fryer, B. 2004. "Breakthrough Ideas for 2004." *Harvard Business Review* 82, pp. 13–14.

Hoque. 2017. www.huffpost.com/entry/thriving-with-mindful-vis_b_4616723

Newport, C. 2016. *Deep Work: Rules for Focused Success in a Distracted Workplace.* New York, NY: Grand Central Publishing.

Russell, J. 2021. "Positive Leadership: It Makes a Difference." *Forbes.*

Sandberg, S., and A. Grant. 2017. *Option B.* Paris: Michel Lafon.

Seligman, M.E. 2006. *Learned Optimism: How to Change Your Mind and Your Life.* New York, NY: Vintage.

Seppala, E. 2015. "Positive Teams Are More Productive." *Harvard Business Review.*

Tugend, A. 2012. "Praise Is Fleeting, but Brickbats We Recall." *New York Times.*

PART 4

What Can I Learn Along the Way?

Learning, Resilience, Listening, Citizenship, and Finances

CHAPTER 14

Learning

LEARNING	MINDSET
	OPPORTUNITY
	CURIOSITY
	CONFIDENCE

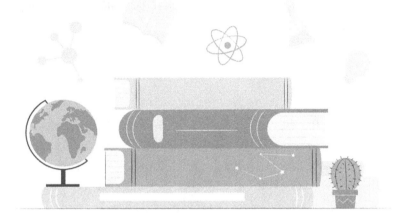

No man ever steps in the same river twice, for it's not the same river and he's not the same man.

—Heraclitis
Greek Philosopher

Introduction

Think back 10 years ago and compare that to who you are today. Think about five years ago and compare that to who you are today. Think about last year, last month, and last week versus who you are today. Think about yesterday versus today. What's the difference between the person you are today and at any point in time in the past? The difference is what we have learned and how we are becoming is a work in process. It's what "sticks" with us in all our life experiences.

We have decisions to make when it comes to learning and it's a decision that plays a huge role in your future success. Will you be someone who burns energy complaining all the time about what didn't go right, or will you be the one who focuses on what you could have done differently to make things better, such that if you ever run into a similar situation you will do better the next time? Will you use every obstacle, every setback, and every experience as an opportunity to learn and grow, or will you simply move through time wondering where all the years went without capturing the growth opportunity?

The decision to be a lifelong learner will make all the difference in the world to you.

Tony's Lessons From Personal Experience

While living in Wichita, Kansas, I learned that hard red winter wheat is planted in the fall and harvested in the spring, eventually being milled into flour and used to make bread. This is completely opposite of the corn/soybean season in the upper Midwest where I was raised. In Torrington, Wyoming, I learned antelope can run as fast as 60 miles per hour and they don't jump over barbed wire fences like deer easily do (they typically run through them, FYI). While traveling in West Texas, I learned the dust they call "caliche" is almost like cement and can prevent water from reaching roots if it gets too bad. While traveling to Germany, I learned that while on the autobahn technically there is no speed limit in some stretches, I am not comfortable above 160 kilometers/hour (100 mph).

In some sense, our lives are unfolding by what we learn each and every day. The opportunities are truly unbounded.

I love the way Hal Moon, a retired John Deere executive, used to talk about knowledge. Hal told thousands of people over the years, "Education produces knowledge, knowledge produces confidence, confidence produces enthusiasm, and enthusiasm is ultimately what sells something!" Yes—knowledge is important, *but not an end in itself.* You must apply it to bring it to life! As the Persian scholar Al Ghazali said, "knowledge without action is wastefulness and action without knowledge is foolishness."

It's sometimes hard to remember that you are a work in progress. You always have been, and you always will be. You are different from morning to night, from day to day, week to week, and year to year. One of the benefits of taking the time to write in a journal is at some point you can look back and observe the growth and changes you can't perceive in the moment. Sometimes you're able to see your growth clearly. While other times, failure may cloud your ability to appreciate how much you've learned.

You push yourself to accomplish the work of this world but forget the engine that creates value in your personal and professional life needs to go in for maintenance occasionally.

The importance of being a lifelong learner can be rediscovered at any point in your career. We live in an age where what we learned 20 or 30 years ago, or even five years ago, isn't necessarily relevant or useful today. It may have been helpful at the time, and it may have made you the person you are today, but if you hold onto it too tightly and don't evolve, odds are the world will move on. Some of your past experiences that were valuable will require you to "unlearn" them to make sure and avoid applying them to new circumstances. Given that new technologies and capabilities are created, shared, and learned at scale on a global basis overnight, we have a fundamentally different world being created "on the fly."

The need to be a lifelong learner as a core part of your life has never been more self-evident. Look at the most successful people you know and think about their approach to learning. Dave Everitt, a mentor of mine once told me, "You need to be confident enough to take on the day and get the job done yet remain humble enough to know you don't have all the answers." I've found this was an excellent way to look at learning throughout my career.

Commit to a lifetime of learning and growing and your career will take off and you will be a great role model for others as well.

Leading Practices

Every day affords us the opportunity to learn—and unlearn—whether through additional formal education or from the experiences and opportunities all around us. Part of this depends on one's curiosity as well as the humility to admit when you don't know enough, when you were wrong, or when you need to evolve and unlearn habits that no longer serve you. Lifelong learners leverage all these opportunities to drive continuous development and improvement. Shape your intentions to learn through:

- Cultivating A Learning Mindset
- Identifying Opportunities
- Building Strategies for Managing Your Learning

Cultivating a Learning Mindset

Author Nick van Dam (2016) puts forth a model of the learning mindset featuring seven key characteristics:

1. A consistent focus on growth;
2. Being a serial master having deep expertise in several areas or skills;
3. Stretching oneself regularly with new challenges;
4. Developing one's brand and network to support learning and open opportunities;
5. Developing a plan and measuring progress toward goals;
6. Focusing on what you love to do and activities that provide you fulfillment;
7. Robust self-care so that a lack of vitality does not inhibit your learning.

The steps above are worthy of revisiting as you gain new experiences in your life. Like climbing a mountain, or even just getting to the top of the next hill in front of you, once there you will be able to see further and have more opportunities to learn and grow that you couldn't possibly have seen in the past. Make it a point to bookmark this part of the book and revisit this from time to time.

Identifying Opportunities

There are many formal ways to engage in continuous learning. You may consider additional degrees, credentials, certifications, and so on offered by universities and institutes, professional associations, or your employer. These options may be more attractive at certain junctures in your career.

However, there is a growing consensus that for some careers, you will need periodic training over an entire career rather than one degree that will last forever.

Informal opportunities to learn also abound. Consider leveraging mindfulness and metacognition when performing work and watching others. For instance, observe how skilled facilitators structure and run a meeting in addition to listening to the content of the session. For content, blogs, podcasts, and newsletters from experts can help you stay abreast of new developments in your professional field or in an area of life where you want to learn more.

Building Strategies for Managing Your Learning

You are responsible for building your own learning and development strategy. Here are some tips to help you manage the process:

- Reserve space on your calendar for learning and growth so it is built into your routine, and you are reminded to devote time to this process.
- Explore how you learn best and what helps you retain new information most effectively. For example, do you prefer learning by doing? Listening? Or reading? Create a mental toolbox where you accumulate information and techniques to aid you in your journey.
- Try something new on a regular basis. If you like an activity, hobby, or topic, then add it to your list of goals.
- As we spend a great deal of time at work, participate actively in learning channels and opportunities. Be especially attentive to opportunities to learn where work is actually happening so you can apply new skills immediately.
- Don't be shy about asking questions and requesting help when you get stuck.

There are lots of opportunities in our life to improve how we learn and grow. Many of these are very personal in nature and build off of your own likes and dislikes when it comes to taking in new information. You will change over time. The world will change over time. What was valid in the past may not be valid in the future. The earlier you get comfortable knowing that you are a work in progress and you have to maintain a constant edge in learning new things, the more successful you will be in your career and the more fulfilling your life will be.

Shared Wisdom: Lessons From the Road

Many of our experts agree that continuous learning has played a role in their successes personally and professionally.

Ross, a cofounder and partner of a wealth management firm, shares the power of investing in yourself and your team at all stage of your career.

> *Investing in yourself by being a continuous learner and in the professional development of your team(s) will pay dividends for many years to come. I received this advice early in my career—late 20s, early 30s as I was transitioning from an individual contributor to a player coach/mentor role.*
>
> —Ross Junge, Cofounder and Partner
> McGill Junge Wealth Management, Iowa, USA

A strategic relationship manager in a major agricultural firm shares advice they received 10 years into their career about the need to always push yourself to learn.

> *Keep pushing to learn and advance yourself, or you will be left behind…ten years into career.*
>
> —Strategic Relationship Manager
> Major agricultural firm, Arkansas, USA

Vikram, a plant manager in the dairy products industry, shares advice on how to test if you are learning and growing enough in your career.

> *Early in my career my mentor said update your resume every 18–24 months, if you didn't have much to add, then you are not learning and growing.*

—Vikram Sriram, Senior Manufacturing Manager
Beyond Meat, Washington, USA

Kelly, a senior executive sales and marketing leader, shares the value of knowing the business and the people, and then when opportunity strikes, show them how much you care about them.

Learn about the business, learn about the people, and when you are given an opportunity to make a difference, show a little hustle.
—Kelly Granatier, Director of Sales
John Deere, Illinois, USA

Bob, a retired senior executive, introduces the concept of reintroducing yourself as new experiences and career opportunities come along. The notion of keeping your personal edge sharp will avoid slipping into routines and career limitations.

Keep reinventing yourself was the best advice. Whether it was new experiences with work or challenges on a personal level. We can all slip into routines that stifle creativity, create lethargy, and limit our view of possibilities. Being a lifelong learner is a way to keep one's personal edge sharp.
—Bob Timmons, Retired Executive
John Deere, Kansas, USA

Than, a director of sales and marketing in the ag industry, shares the power of stretching beyond your comfort zones to expand your experience and career opportunities.

Stretch outside of your comfort zone in order to learn and grow; received about three years into my career at a point when I was wanting to stay in the areas I knew well.
—Than Hartsock, Director, Corn and Soybean Production
Systems
John Deere, Illinois, USA

Kiley, a president and CEO of a nonprofit, shares a powerful story from his family about the powerful combination of having the courage to stretch, combined with the rapid mastery and quick learning skills to adopt. Taken together, these attributes can lead to surprising results.

When I was considering applying for my first job in economic development and chamber of commerce work after several years as a journalist, I asked my dad his thoughts. He told me that I should apply. When I argued that I didn't know anything about the field, he pointed his finger at me and said, "You bullshit them in the boardroom, and you learn as fast as you can." I realized at that moment that was how my dad had survived as a 24-year-old hospital CEO. He didn't know what he was doing, but he was courageous enough to bullshit them in the boardroom and humble and hungry enough to learn as fast as he could.

—Kiley Miller, President and CEO
Trees Forever, Iowa, USA

In addition to acquiring knowledge and building skills, experience also plays a vital role in your learning if you take the time to analyze and reflect. This is the space for planning and serial mastery. And we see that the occasional misstep can also generate great lessons.

Learn by making mistakes through courageous decisions!
—Production System Programs Manager
John Deere, Kaiserslautern, Germany

Bob, a retired executive in the financial services industry, underscores the reality we can learn from every situation. Over time as these experiences accumulate so will your capabilities.

You can learn from every situation and especially every interaction with leaders. Add the skills that you found helpful or appealing to your toolbox for the future. This was very early in my career.
—Bob Larson, Retired Executive
John Deere, Illinois, USA

Nathan, a vice president of an integrated marketing firm, highlights the power of learning from failures, even more than our successes, and how using advisers can enhance and accelerate our learning.

We are quick to share our successes; however, so much more is learned from our failures that can drive future growth and success when we have a strong analysis of what led to the failure and what can we learn from it. Allowing trusted advisers into this area allows for another perspective that we may not have.

—Nathan Johnson, Vice President
Strategic America, Iowa, USA

A Chief Information Security Officer shares the power of using the quiet times to cultivate learning and growth.

A mentor once told me "Our lives are complicated and challenging, but there are times during your career where things are 'quiet' allowing additional time for you to learn a skill, build the right relationships, or invest in capability that allows you to become an expert. The world needs more experts. It is critical that you identify those 'quiet' times in your life and make the most of them."

—Chief Information Security Officer
Fortune 100 firm, Illinois, USA

Aaron shares his personal journey of building his career and learning by treating his career like pieces of pie, and how this led to personal and professional growth, and ultimately, more happiness in his life.

Treat your career like a piece of pie. Then eat the whole pie. In my first year of a 20+ year stint, I asked a respected RVP about his career path in hopes of gaining insight into how to get to be CEO. Because, of course, every first-year employee thinks they can be CEO. The leader went on to explain that each piece was a different part of the business, claims, underwriting, sales, office experience, field experience, etc. And that to succeed, it was critical to understand the details of how the business is run. I took that advice to heart for some reason, probably because I didn't have a better strategy, and set out littering my career path with purposeful change across all disciplines. I soon realized that each discipline I "mastered" was enabling me to master the next and I quickly gained unique perspectives giving me a competitive advantage. These perspectives helped me bridge knowledge gaps and silos across organizations while building a large, informal support network that became invaluable in getting things done. It also instilled in me a skill set that I still leverage daily in my career: a focus on ROI to assess every job/role/activity back to the business impact and why we exist in the first place. It seems like a silly little analogy, but it had a significant impact on my personal and professional life. It allowed me to learn, grow, and remain challenged for 20 years. Most importantly, it allowed me to contribute business value and help others, which in turn gave me happiness.

—Aaron Sands, Technical Product Management Leader
Corteva Agriscience, Iowa, USA

Tom, a retired executive, shares a story about making mistakes and learning that had a profound impact on his career and outlook on learning from our mistakes.

I was driving down I-35 from home in Dallas. The day before I got a phone call from a dealer who asked me a pricing question. Rather than pull over and check my answer, or ask if I could get back to him, I recalled the Finance Bulletin and to the best of my recollection I responded. That night when I was back home, I looked up the Finance Bulletin and realized I made a $5,000 mistake on the information I gave the dealer.

Now back to the drive. Bryan is a good three-hour drive, and I would always leave by 6:00 to beat the morning traffic and be there by 9:00. I knew I could always reach my Division Sales Manager in the office by 6:30 a.m.

I called expecting the worst! I explained my phone call from the day before and the commitment I made to the dealer. There was silence for what seemed like several minutes and was probably only seconds. My manager asked me to call him back on my drive home while he figured out what we were going to do.

In my dealing with the dealer in Bryan that day my thoughts kept going back to my phone call I had to make and the possibilities of what might come from it.

On the way home, I made the call and asked what I should do about the mistake I made.

In his slow delivery and Texas drawl, he said "Hughes, we're not going to do anything about it. If that's what you told the dealer he gets, then that's what we'll give him." He continued, "I just wanted to see if your $5,000 mistake was going to affect the price of our stock today."

Now there was silence on my side of the phone.

He ended with "I bet you never make that mistake again. Don't worry about it and you have a safe drive home."

Later in my career, when I had the chance to supervise others, I drew upon those words by telling them not to be afraid to make mistakes. We learn from it, don't make the mistakes again, and move on.

—Tom Hughes, Retired Executive
John Deere, Texas, USA

Reflections: What's Your Story?

1. What are your main insights/takeaways from the chapter at this moment?

_____

_____

_____

_____

_____

_____

_____

_____

_____

2. What are one to three goals/intentions you would like to set for yourself?

_____

_____

_____

_____

_____

_____

_____

_____

_____

Going Further: Questions, Readings, and References

Discussion Questions

14.1   Tony talked about Hal Moon's formula that goes from education and knowledge leads to confidence and enthusiasm. When in your life have you felt particularly passionate, confident, and enthused upon learning something new? How can this inform your learning mindset?

14.2   Leaders often identify their greatest learning in times of failure, not success. Think back to some of your failures you have experienced. How did you handle them from a lifelong learning perspective?

14.3   Which of the seven steps to cultivating a learning mindset resonates with you the most?

14.4   When was the last time you tried something new? How often do you expose yourself to new things? What can you do in the next week to explore new ideas?

14.5   Think about where you were five or even 10 years ago. How have you changed during this time? Now think about the next five or 10 years of your life and the opportunity you have to learn and grow new things? What are you willing to do to ensure you optimize your learning and growth in the future?

Suggested Reading

Brazer, B. 2015. *A Curious Mind: The Secret to a Bigger Life*. New York, NY: Simon & Schuster Paperbacks.

Clark, D. 2021. *The Long Game: How to Be a Long-Term Thinker in a Short-Term World*. Boston, MA: Harvard Business Review Press.

Goldsmith, M. 2010. *What Got You Here Won't Get You There: How Successful People Become Even More Successful*. Profile books.

Grant, A. 2021. *Think Again: The Power of Knowing What You Don't Know*. New York, NY: Viking.

Reference

van Dam, N. 2016. *Learn or Lose*. Breukelen, Netherlands: Nyenrode Publishing.

CHAPTER 15

Resilience

RESILIENCE

WELLNESS
PURPOSE
SELF-CARE
SUPPORT

When I kept failing at meeting goals in my job, I wanted to quit. At the time I thought this job was not for me. My mentor and my family reminded me why I wanted to challenge myself and that I cannot quit when things are bad. I need to fix the problem and only then I can leave. I am so glad I stayed because I learned so much through all the failures.

—Morgan Jia, Engineering Manager
John Deere, California, USA

Introduction

You've been goal-oriented and you seek to achieve ambitious outcomes in your life. You've put yourself in a great position to succeed. You have a great strategy and a solid plan to execute the strategy. You've even assembled the appropriate resources and support and dedicated yourself by working harder than you have ever worked in your life. Seems like you have checked all the boxes for success and what only remains is the time to get the job done. Despite all of this, failure is upon you and you are left wondering what went wrong?

It is a difficult realization when you've given everything you possibly can to a cause and still failed. At that very moment, we can build another core competency of life: Resilience.

Resilience says that no matter what comes your way, you will not be defeated. You will put in the best of your abilities, and you will adjust and adapt as necessary, but you will not be defeated. A friend and flyfishing guide, Kea Hause, helped me learn this lesson while we were on the Roaring Fork River one day. We hadn't caught a fish all day, but Kea would not accept it. He taught me resilience is the space between giving everything you can possibly give *"and then giving a little bit more."* He simply would never accept we have done all we could do to catch a fish and yet every time we found a way before the end of the day!

Resilience says more about your character than it does about how strong you are. You simply keep trying in the moment. One step further, one day more, one more try. Resilience is the fuel that keeps you going when hard work runs out.

Tony's Lessons From Personal Experience

Some of the most emotional experiences in our lives will come during times of failure and self-doubt. Everyone has them in their life, but especially so for those who are ambitious and trying to accomplish things in this world. Inevitable failures and shortcomings bring intense feeling of self-doubt but also serve as a springboard to resiliency. Strangely, I don't think you can discover resiliency without going through failure and self-doubt. It's part of the process. It's not fun, but it's the way it is.

By the time I was 16, I had done my fair share of stupid things. Most of this was not having the self-awareness of how self-centered I was and being blind to the damage I was doing to the people around me. I'm sure by the time I was 16, some people had written a script for my life and it wasn't necessarily a positive one. That's when my older brother Marty gave me his copy of *See You at the Top* by Zig Ziglar and I did something really unusual at the time. *I read it.*

One particular line spoke to me—"*You don't drown by falling into deep water, you drown by staying there.*" From that moment on, my past did not equal my future. It didn't matter what happened in my past, from that very moment on I could rewrite a script for my future. It was an extremely liberating feeling that energized me and to this day influences how I look at the world. I can make a mistake, but it only kills me if I stay in that mistake and don't move on. "Be a goldfish" as Ted Lasso would recommend, that is, have a short memory when you make mistakes.

As my career took shape, those words helped me when I was confronted with challenging situations. I will never forget receiving the news that my job was being eliminated. This has occurred three times over the last 34 years. I was very fortunate each time to be able to be offered other roles in the company. Sometimes this meant moving to take on a new job elsewhere in the company and uprooting my family. Other times it meant a change in pay and benefits. Still other times it meant taking on new and unfamiliar responsibilities. *Sometimes it meant all three!* Looking back, it was an emotional journey every time, and sacrifices were made each time to maintain my relationship with the company.

I also was grateful because I know things don't always work out to stay with the company during times of change. Maybe in a sense during these times I metaphorically fell into the deep end of the company pool, but it was up to me how I was going to react to it.

Each time I searched my soul for what I wanted to do in the world, weighed my value proposition on what I believed versus the feedback I was getting from others, and sought to learn from each of these experiences. As much as I disliked these parts of my career, each time I came away stronger, more resilient, and more motivated at the end. Again, it sure didn't feel like that at the moment. It's also good to learn you can survive these types of events and live to fight another day.

I was one of the lucky ones, but I know there are so many others whose jobs were eliminated and through no fault of their own didn't have a way to extend their careers. These are all great people, friends, and professionals with tremendous skills, leadership, and growth potential. It taught me a valuable lesson: I can be having a great career, only to run into a buzz saw at any moment and find myself on my own.

You will no doubt face challenging moments in your career. Earlier in your career, it may seem easy to jump to a new opportunity or pivot to a different career. But things tend to change once you have a mortgage, a family, or have built up a certain level of expertise in one domain or another. Switching costs are harder and taking the time to build resiliency in your career will be important. Make sure at all times during your journey that you are always running downhill, leaning into progress, and staying positive and constructive no matter what the possible outcomes are.

Leading Practices

There is so much fantastic research accumulated over many years that identifies very specific practices to develop personal and professional resilience. You could spend years reviewing all the relevant literature and still not be close to scratching the surface. This book focuses on those key elements of resilience that can help create a successful career and a more fulfilling life. Therefore, it is important to identify those elements of resilience that support each of those aspects. The American Psychological Association (APA) defines resilience as

The process of adapting well in the face of adversity, trauma, tragedy, threats, or significant sources of stress—such as family and relationship problems, serious health problems, or workplace and financial stressors.

—APA, 2020

Following from the leadership and guidance of the APA (2020), the following leading practices can help support resilience across both personal and professional dimensions. Furthermore, many of these dimensions of wellness align to very specific chapters within this book—and that is by design!

- Know Thyself: Assess your Resilience
- Connections
- Foster Wellness

- Purpose
- Embrace Healthy Thoughts

Know Thyself: Assess Your Resilience

A powerful tool to build resilience is to assess your current state of resilience. One accepted and validated methodology is the Connor–Davidson Resilience Scale developed by psychiatrist Kathryn Connor and Duke University Professor of Psychiatry and Behavioral Science, Jonathan Davidson. This scale provides a baseline assessment of your current level of resilience, which can change over time. It measures the following components (Riopel 2022):

- The ability to adapt to change
- The ability to deal with what comes along
- The ability to cope with stress
- The ability to stay focused and think clearly
- The ability to not get discouraged in the face of failure
- The ability to handle unpleasant feelings such as anger, pain, or sadness

By starting with an accurate assessment of your current state, you can devise a productive plan to increase your resilience in one or more key areas as outlined below.

Connections

First, it is critically important to create and protect space for social connections. As mentioned previously, our species is hardwired for social connection. Therefore, we need to intentionally develop relationships with those individuals and groups that help meet this need for ourselves. These connections can be personal or professional. We all find purpose in different ways. Some may find it at work with a particularly meaningful project, or others may realize purpose and connection through joining a group (e.g., sports club, hobby interest-group, or volunteer organization).

The most important thing is to ensure you have the appropriate breath and/or depth of connections that contribute to your overall social wellness and resilience.

Foster Wellness

As discussed in *Well-Being* (Chapter 4), there are at least eight generally accepted dimensions of wellness. While we won't repeat all the previous leading practices, it is worthwhile to mention that taking care of your physical and emotional needs is paramount to creating resilience. For instance, practicing mindfulness through meditation can be a powerful way to focus your mind, body, and spirit to support overall wellness. Additionally, research suggests that cultivating self-respect or self-compassion is another critical component to overall health and wellness (Newman 2016).

Purpose

As described in *Purpose* (Chapter 5), identifying your core purpose is critically important to a successful career and more fulfilling life. Pursuing your purpose can be incredibly rewarding. And it can take a lot of time, or for some people, it becomes apparent very quickly. Helping others and/or servant leadership is a very common purpose that balances individualism with altruism.

Embrace Healthy Thoughts

This dimension of resilience is built around the idea that we generally benefit from maintaining an optimistic and hopeful outlook. It's important to keep things in perspective so that we are able to accept change and/or learn from our past. Furthermore, cultivating forgiveness for all of those around us is generally a better alternative than maintaining a corrosive grudge.

Final Note on Seeking Help

We are all sincerely dedicated to developing resilience and positive mental health. We recognize the "culture of pulling yourself up by your bootstraps" is strong within our society. However, we can't always do it alone—and in fact, we rarely achieve anything without the help and assistance of others. If you ever feel that you need additional support, we strongly recommend reaching out to a certified mental health professional to help you walk along the journey. In our lives, it has been proven indispensable when faced with periods of both profound stress and joy.

Shared Wisdom: Lessons From the Road

Resilience can be called the backbone of our career, keeping us steady during stormy moments and keeping us moving forward when everything is pushing against us. Finding the power in all of us and developing a sense of resilience is something our community of leaders had a lot of advice on.

Nils, a president of an automotive technology division, shares the powerful advice of taking responsibility for failures but then through accountability and learning, move on.

> *Dealing with own failure, taking accountability was hard to establish, but the good old values of honesty and transparency did solve it. Stand up for your failures and mistakes, be truthful about it, speak about it—and move on.*
> —Nils Jaeger, President of Volvo Automation Solutions
> Volvo Group, Goteborg, Sweden

Aaron, a chief technology officer of a software development firm, shares his experience in learning more from his failures than any other outcome. Notable is his observation that it doesn't have to be *your failure* in order to learn from failure.

> *I've learned more from failure than any other form. In some cases that was being a leader in underperforming projects with high stakes. In other times it would be watching how other leaders make mistakes and learning from them. Failure is a tough but effective teacher.*
> —Aaron Senneff, Chief Technology Officer
> Pushpay, Colorado, USA

Jena, a general manager at John Deere, shares the power of believing in yourself and how this leads to strength and resilience.

From my executive coach of 11 years, I learned that courage is about believing in yourself and others and knowing you have the strength and resilience to succeed.

—Jena Holtberg-Benge, General Manager
John Deere Reman, Missouri, USA

Leonardo, a director of technology, shares how he would never want to change his past decisions because of the value he received from them by way of a more resilient capability in his career going forward.

I think that I made some mistakes in some early decisions in my career, but I will never want to change my past decisions because they make me more resilient and what I am at my career today is a result of my past decisions and I like where I am today.

—Leonardo Chechi, Director of Technology
Cruzeiro do Sul Grãos, Brazil

Doerthe, a mid-career executive at a workplace specialty firm in Sweden, shares that one aspect of being truly resilient is having a strong support group and finding the "right" people who will be there to support you.

You might be very lucky at one time with a manager or a teacher who encourages and motivates you which will enable you to exceed your performance above what you might have expected. I had a wonderful Swedish teacher which enabled me to learn the language and be fluent after two years.

As simple as that another time you might need to work with a manager or a peer that causes you the biggest frustration ever and kills all your motivation and willingness to perform because the person has insufficient people managing skills and prejudice related to your gender or education.

So the conclusion is that the biggest problems but also the greatest achievements are always related and linked to people that surround you and you work with.

How to resolve it? Go and find the right people that encourage you and build a strong shield and resilience against those who don't want to support you and make your life a trouble. It is not worth it to spend time and energy to fight them. Invest the energy in developing your strengths and changing your life for yourself.

—Doerthe Zick, Workplace Expert
Workplaces for Industries, Gnoso, Sweden

Laetitia, a digital product owner, shares her personal journey and how critical it was for her to always be fighting for herself, and never give up, which led to personal and professional growth.

The biggest problem I faced was at the beginning of my career or should I say I was struggling to start a career. Initially, I wanted to become a doctor but my parents couldn't finance my studies so I left home, found a part time job as cashier and attended biology courses at university in parallel. I graduated a few years later with a Bachelor of Biology Degree but then couldn't find any job in my field, the marketplace, especially in labs, was fully saturated. To subsist, I looked for a job outside of my field. I started with short missions as a temp worker for insurance companies and banks in Luxembourg and continued to look for a better job in parallel. Next, I found a Management Assistant position. I didn't know anything about computers or IT at that time. As part of my new role, I decided to learn Microsoft Office more deeply. With my scientific background, I liked it and continued with databases and programming languages. This allowed me the opportunity of working closer with the project team who delivered some IT programs. I was feeling more and more knowledgeable in IT so looked for a proper IT job. I was recruited as IT Developer and worked for the European Commission. Despite my very basic English, I visited some Eastern Europe countries (Bulgaria, Latvia, Slovakia) to deploy some IT programs and train end users. When I'm asked today "how did someone who studied biology end up leading an IT team?" my answer is very simple: I've been fighting, I never gave up! I have been playing table tennis at the top level for 20 years and had the chance to travel around the world to play competition. I visited Russia, Belgium, Austria, Germany, Israel... With sport, I learned to win, to lose, to cope with pressure, and became resilient. I met many challenges during my career and also in my personal life. I believe sport and competition taught me how to go over those obstacles.

—Laetitia Baratelli, Digital Product Owner

John Deere Financial, Luxembourg

Reflections: What's Your Story?

1. What are your main insights/takeaways from the chapter at this moment?

_____

_____

_____

_____

_____

_____

_____

_____

2. What are one to three goals/intentions you would like to set for yourself?

_____

_____

_____

_____

_____

_____

_____

_____

_____

Going Further: Questions, Readings, and References

Discussion Questions

15.1 Tony mentions Zig Ziglar's quote "You don't drown by falling into deep water. You drown by staying there." When have you "fallen into deep water" in your life? What was the outcome? What did you learn and take forward from this experience?

15.2 Aaron Senneff mentions "Failure is a tough but effective teacher." What does this mean to you given your experiences with failure in the past? How does this shape your thinking about your future relationship with failure?

15.3 Resiliency means adapting and overcoming challenges in your life. Where are you at in your life on the Connor–Davidson Resilience Scale?

15.4 Thinking back to *Purpose and Vision* (Chapter 5)—how can having a strong purpose and vision aid you in living a more resilient life?

15.5 Think about a time when you came up short in your personal life and let people you care about down in some way. Did this differ in any way from how you view professional shortcomings? When emotions come into play more, how does this impact your perspective?

Suggested Reading

David, S. 2016. *Emotional Agility: Get Unstuck, Embrace Change, and Thrive in Work and Life*. New York, NY: Avery.

Duckworth, A. 2016. *Grit: The Power of Passion and Perseverance*. New York, NY: Scribner.

Hanson, R. 2018. *Resilient: How to Grow an Unshakable Core of Calm, Strength, and Happiness*. New York, NY: Harmony.

References

APA. 2020. www.apa.org/topics/resilience

Connor–Davidson Resilience Scale. n.d. www.cd-risc.com/

Newman. 2016. https://greatergood.berkeley.edu/article/item/five_science_backed_
strategies_to_build_resilience

Riopel, L. 2022. https://positivepsychology.com/connor-davidson-brief-resilience-
scale/

CHAPTER 16

Listening

LISTENING

W.A.I.T.
SILENCE
ENGAGE
UNDERSTAND

Never miss a good chance to shut up.

—Will Rogers
American film actor

Introduction

One of the most important competences in the business world is communication skills. How well do you present? How well do you articulate yourself in the written word? How well do you handle yourself in group settings when the need for teamwork is high? Can you get your point across clearly and crisply? These are all important aspects of our work, no doubt. But there is one other huge part of communication that is often less understood and even less spoken about: The art and skill of listening.

Most people are horrible listeners as they most often listen only enough to be able to provide a reply. The act of listening is over as soon as they start rehearsing their response in their mind. Finally, listening is reduced to the patience it takes to identify a point in the conversation where you can show the room how smart you are.

Personal development gold mines exist for those willing to truly master the skill of listening. Listening to what people are saying sometimes requires us to actively clear our mind to hear every word they say without worrying about how you will respond. It will also open you up to what they are not saying but "how" they are saying it—nonverbal cues that also inform you about what someone is telling you.

If you truly master listening skills, you will have a gift that never stops giving.

Tony's Lessons From Personal Experience

I love to flyfish. Over the last 30 years, I've found that if I want to get into a "zen" state just put me on a stream for a day and before I know it the day has gone blissfully by. If I am fishing by myself, I've gotten into the habit of spending 15 minutes watching the stream before making my first cast. I'm sure if a passerby would observe me during these first 15 minutes, I would look like just another guy staring at a stream. But these 15 minutes are the most critical part of my day. These first 15 minutes have more to say about my success than the most perfectly executed cast all day long.

I watch the water for how it flows. I look for seams of fast- and slow-moving water knowing that fish lay in the slow-moving water to save energy while waiting for food in the faster water. I watch for any movement on top of the water to see if there are any insects hatching that might signal a particular food supply for that stream. One way to know an experienced fly fisher from a beginner is the experienced fly fisher only decides what fly to use after watching the water for a while. I watch for underwater flashes of color that might reveal an actively feeding fish on the stream bottom. I review the streambed and determine the best place to start without increasing the chances of spooking any fish. Lastly, I take in the environment around me and make note of obstacles I need to be careful to avoid: a tree branch in my back cast, a logjam that creates faster moving water, or a steep bank indicating deeper water. I take note of the weather and where my shadow is and where it will be as I enter the water.

I even think about how I might land a fish if I hook one, and where it would be easiest to net them.

Every detail counts and most of what is important is determined in those first 15 minutes.

Listening is a lot like those first 15 minutes of fishing. You are taking in information. You are sensing what is going on around you. You are actively observing everything there is to be observed. You are focused and intentional. You are not only hearing and seeing and feeling, but you are understanding and extending this understanding to make a difference in your life when the time does come to act.

Equally important is what I am *not* doing. I'm not trying to impose my will on the stream. I'm not thinking through the years of experience I have and starting my day with a set plan of action. I'm not tying on a fly at my vehicle that worked for years in similar streams. I'm not taking immediate action the moment I see a fish. I'm not making assumptions about what I think I should experience on the river. I'm not making judgments about what other similar rivers have been like and applying them to this stream. Sometimes taking time to observe a river *is actually fishing a river.*

It's easy for me to talk about flyfishing, Zen, and things that carry me away in the pursuit of my passions. But what does this have to do with the rest of the time and how might this relate to building a successful career and a more fulfilling life?

Listening is a massively underrated skill that some people never master. We are taught in school and at work how important "Presentation Skills" are. We are told how important communication skills are, and then we are presented with a plethora of options that focus on talking skills. For most of my career, the message pounded into me was that communication meant improving my presentation skills. Ninety-nine percent of the training I received on communication was about how to improve *executive presence*—what to wear, appropriate business protocols, or speaking with impact, and so on....

The one exception to this was Paul Axtell's seminar on critical conversations called "Foundations" in 1994. He said to me, "the quality of your life will be dictated by the quality of your conversations" and the "quality of your conversations often comes down to your listening skills." It was a powerful message and I've tried to remember this standard ever since I took that seminar.

You and I live in an increasingly noisy world. I've been told that today is the slowest day of the rest of my life and I believe it. Twenty-four-hour news cycles, social media that never sleeps, and a world where news travels globally with lightning speed are all parts of this noise. There is no shortage of distractions. Couple this with increasing workloads, family needs, community commitments, and on and on it goes. Time's arrow seems to always point to more complexity and distractions.

Take the time to get good at listening. *It will make you look like a genius.* It will make you stand out. People will say you are wise beyond your years simply because you are paying attention.

Leading Practices

Research supports the idea that listening is a critical component of successful leadership. In fact, it is estimated that good (or bad) listening skills can account for up to 40 percent of a leader's assessed performance (Bradbury 2015). According to one study, good listening helps (1) build stronger relationships, (2) develop greater trust, (3) promote effective collaboration within teams, and (4) ultimately enhances greater productivity, creativity, and innovation (Westover 2020). Here are some leading practices that can help you develop your own listening skills:

- W.A.I.T.: Why Am I Talking?
- Silence is Golden: Be Comfortable in the Quiet
- Active Listening: A Self-Assessment

W.A.I.T.: Why Am I Talking?

Finally, in a chapter about listening, we believe the W.A.I.T. decision-tree chart could be one of the most important (and hilarious) practical tools for improving your listening. By following this chart, you can determine if talking is required. Furthermore, all paths end with the kind reminder to "Be concise." So, in the spirit of W.A.I.T., why are we still talking! Just use the chart and see how it goes!

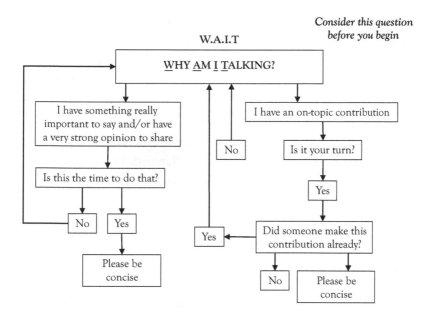

*Consider this question
before you begin*

Silence Is Golden: Be Comfortable in the Quiet

Maybe, it is a tad ironic that Alfred Brendel, a musician, often reminded the world that "The word listen contains the same letters as the word silent?" Just like Tony's silent study of the river, the role and influence of silence in our lives is profound. Silence, downtime, and resting our senses gives us the capacity to be present and listen more deeply when necessary. According to the Cleveland Clinic, silence can positively affect both physical and mental processes. Physically, it lowers blood pressure, decreases heart rate, steadies your breathing, reduces muscle tension, and increases focus and cognition. Mentally, silence allows for self-reflection, increases awareness of what matters most, and cultivates mindfulness (Cleveland Clinic 2020).

In the United States and other Western nations, we are generally less comfortable with silence than our Eastern friends and colleagues from Japan or China. In our classes with undergraduates, it takes about three to four seconds of silence before someone is compelled to fill the silence to reduce the tension. One famous negotiation between a U.S. company and a Japanese company saw the U.S. team make an opening offer, while the Japanese team remained silent. The U.S. team reduced their offer to please their counterparts, but the Japanese team remained silent. Finally, the U.S. negotiators reduced their offer one last time and the Japanese graciously accepted without saying a word. Asked later, the Japanese company responded they would have gladly accepted the first offer, but their U.S. colleagues kept reducing the price without their needing to do anything at all! Whether you are in a high-stakes negotiation, or having a coaching conversation with a friend, remember to practice using silence to allow sufficient time and space for a worthwhile response.

Active Listening: A Self-Assessment

Once you've started the journey of mindful listening, you could take it to the next level by practicing active listening. If someone is listening actively, they understand themselves as active participants in mutual dialogue and not just passive recipients of verbal data. Some of the following characteristics are good indicators of active listening:

- Show the speaker you are interested by maintaining appropriate eye contact.
- Balance engaged listening with short note-taking to remember key points.
- Remain nonjudgmental to what is being shared—this enables thoughtful responses at the appropriate time.
- Plan ahead so that you can minimize distractions (e.g., phone, e-mail, dog, etc.). This is especially important in virtual interactions when the desire to multitask is strongest.
- Attempt to relate to the person "behind those eyes." This is one of our favorites and it means that we should always be attuned to the emotional cues underlying the spoken words. Everyone is going through something we know nothing about and the best active listeners leverage both their emotional quotient (EQ) and intelligence quotient (IQ) to support all aspects of those around us.

With practice, active listening becomes second nature. Where are you on your listening developmental journey? Here is a sample Active Listening Self-Assessment that can identify your strengths and possible opportunities to develop your skills (Harvard Business School 2004).

Active listening self-assessment

Are You an Active Listener?
Coaches who listens actively tend to get the most out of their coaching discussions and tend to be better coaches overall. Use this self-assessment to think about how actively you listen and to identify areas for improvement. Check the box next to the number in the column that best describes your listening habits.

While someone is talking, I:	Usually	Sometimes	Rarely
Plan how I'm going to respond	1	3	5
Keep eye contact with the speaker	5	3	1
Take notes as appropriate	5	3	1
Notice the feeling behind the words	5	3	1
Find myself thinking about other things while the person is talking	1	3	5
Face the person who is talking	5	3	1
Watch for significant body language (expressions, gestures, etc.)	5	3	1
Control fidgeting or other distracting habits	5	3	1
Interrupt the speaker to make a point	1	3	5
Am distracted by other demands on my time	1	3	5
Listen to the message without immediately judging or evaluating it	5	3	1
Ask questions to get more information and encourage the speaker to continue	5	3	1
Repeat in my own words what I've just heard to ensure understanding	5	3	1
Total for each column:			
Grand total:			

Scoring:
49–65 = You are an active listener.
31–48 = You are a good listener with room for improvement.
13–30 = You need to focus on improving your listening skills.

If you received a score between 13 and 48, develop a plan for strengthening your active listening skills. Write your ideas in the space below.

_____

_____

Shared Wisdom: Lessons From the Road

Listening was easily one of the most common pieces of wisdom to emerge from our community of experts. The Greek Stoic philosopher Epictetus was one of the first to note: "We have two ears and one mouth so that we can listen twice as much as we speak." Here are some good stories about how our experts put that lesson into practice.

A consultant from a major consulting firm shared their advice about the simple, yet powerful, behavior of listening without thinking of how you will respond.

Listen without thinking about your response. You'll be surprised how much more you learn and how much more inclined people will be to listen to you.

—Consultant
Boston Consulting Group, Illinois, USA

Abhay, managing director of a financial services firm of a major Fortune 100 company in India, shares his journey of professional growth and how pivotal it was for him to learn listening skills in his professional development.

The best advice I received was on patience, perseverance, and importance of group decisioning. I was transitioning from a manager in small organization with fewer cross functions to a manager in large organization with multiple cross-functional and cross-geographical stakeholders. That was about 10 years back. With that advice, I realized the importance of listening, appreciating diverse viewpoints, evaluating, and including it during execution. This helped me anchor firmly to organization and people.

—Abhay Dhokte, Managing Director
John Deere Financial, Maharashtra, India

Peter, a retired college professor, shares how impactful interacting with another senior leader has been when it came to his leadership style and in particular his listening skills.

Very early on in our career, we worked for an energetic woman whose advice to us came in how she operated with us, as staff. She was always there to listen. When a problem was presented, she was immediately on it working a solution. She was, perhaps, one of the most effective leaders we have seen, and taught us A LOT by watching her operate. We have modeled our entire career in higher education after her listening leadership and style.

—Peter L. Smith, Retired
University of Dubuque, New Hampshire, USA

John, a director in a major financial services division of a Fortune 100 company, reiterates the age-old lesson on the value of having two ears and one mouth.

You have two ears and one mouth for a reason, listen and the solutions to real issues will become evident.
—John Winger, Director, Retail Credit Delivery
John Deere Financial, Iowa, USA

Many members of our community shared that listening not only helped solve important specific challenges, it also had the added benefit of increasing buy-in for the eventual solution. When you're caught up in the moment, learning to pause and listen can be difficult. But these experts identify active listening as one of their most important leadership tools.

An engineering manager of a major manufacturing engineering firm shares very powerful advice about knowing when to talk and when to listen. Notable is the wisdom gained from listening to truly build support in the final analysis or decision.

The biggest problem I faced in my career was learning the importance of buy-in and not always taking the last word in a conversation. Solving technical problems comes naturally for me and my biggest contributions to the world certainly fall into that category. However, it is easy to erase months and years of technical achievement by simply not recognizing when it's no longer your time to talk. In the end, no one really cares how well you can solve problems if you do not also sincerely appreciate and accept the contributions of others along the way. Most importantly, you must be self-aware when you start coming across too strong in defending your own position and relax and listen.
—Manager, Product Test and Evaluation
Major manufacturing engineering services, USA

Chris, a retired sales and marketing executive, shares his experiences struggling with active listening, and the power and growth that came from improving in this area.

Early in my career, I struggled with active listening. Due to both over-confidence or in some cases a lack of confidence, rather than listening to an individual or group to gather all of the facts, I would place my energy and focus on developing my response before having received all of the information/facts. I would provide a response before all information was received. In some cases, working with upset customers, I would interrupt the customer before they fully explained their situation/problem. As you might suspect, this created some challenges with both my working and personal relationships. I struggled with this until I finally recognized this behavior gap through mistakes I made, and training I received focused on active listing, and direct/strong feedback from others. I recognized active listening was the key to not only developing strong working relationships, regardless of whether they are work or personal relationships. Active listening allowed me to respond with fact-based solutions and assisted in developing strong relationships.

—Chris Ohnysty, Retired Executive
John Deere, Iowa, USA

Reflections: What's Your Story?

1. What are your main insights/takeaways from the chapter at this moment?

_____

_____

_____

_____

_____

_____

_____

_____

2. What are one to three goals/intentions you would like to set for yourself?

_____

_____

_____

_____

_____

_____

_____

_____

_____

Going Further: Questions, Readings, and References

Discussion Questions

16.1   Tony talked about his experience in "listening" to a stream before fishing it. When are you at your best when it comes to listening? How can you make every conversation better?

16.2   Paul Axtell advises us "The quality of our life depends upon the quality of our conversations." In the next 24 hours, before every conversation, take the conscious step to say you are going to be a master listener. How did that feel and what did you learn?

16.3   Test out the W.A.I.T. (Why Am I Talking?) model on a few conversations in the next couple of days. How did this change the quality of your conversation?

16.4   The letters in "listen" include the same letters in "silent." Think about how you use silence in your life and how it impacts you physically (e.g., blood pressure) and mentally.

16.5   If you had to describe your preferred style, would you say you are an introvert or an extravert? How does this preference influence your ability to listen?

16.6   What is the role of technology in helping you listen to others? Conversely, what is the role of technology is preventing you from being able to listen to others?

Suggested Reading

Goulston, M. 2010. *Just Listen: Discover the Secret to Getting Through to Absolutely Anyone.* New York, NY: American Management Association.

Murphy, K. 2019. *You're Not Listening: What You're Missing and Why it Matters.* New York, NY: Celadon Books.

Nichols, M.P., and M.B. Straus. 2021. *The Lost Art of Listening: How Learning to Listen Can Improve Relationships.* 3rd ed. New York, NY: The Guilford Press.

References

Bradbury. 2015. www.weforum.org/agenda/2015/10/why-successful-people-are-great-listeners/

Cleveland Clinic. 2020. https://health.clevelandclinic.org/why-you-need-more-silence-in-your-life/

Harvard Business School Publishing. 2004. Active Listening Self-Assessment.

Westover. 2020. www.forbes.com/sites/forbescoachescouncil/2020/08/17/the-power-of-listening/?sh=b319bd116a38

CHAPTER 17

Citizenship

CITIZENSHIP

DOING
BEING
SHARING
CARING
SERVING

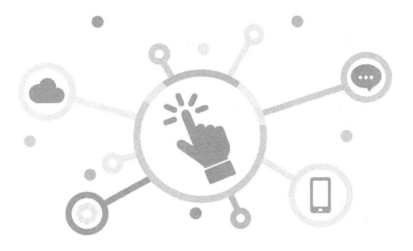

For of those to whom much is given much is required.

—John F. Kennedy
35th U.S. President

For unto whomsoever much is given, of him shall be much required.

—Luke 12:48
Christian Bible

Introduction

The goal of this book is to help you build the right foundation so that you can lead a good career and a more fulfilling life. Building the right foundation will help you do more, be more, and accomplish more than you ever dreamed. Once in place, you can continue to add to your foundation as your career and life experiences expand.

Knowing yourself and managing yourself is a big part of who you will become in your life. But who you become to the outside world is also a major part of your identity. This outward identity—or citizenship—defines who you are and how you want to participate in society. How will you contribute to the common good? How will you help contribute to others in your community? In the world?

This chapter touches on becoming a solid citizen as we seek to build a strong foundation for our life.

Tony's Lessons From Personal Experience

Sam Allen, retired CEO of Deere and Company, used to say he required three things of every employee when he visited operations. The first was to understand our strategy and do all we could to help execute it. Second, become the very best you can be at whatever your role is. Invest in yourself and grow your career. Third, he stressed, was to give back to your community. He not only told this to thousands of employees over the course of his 40-year career he personally lived by his own words by dedicating personal time in his home community as well as far-off communities in programs to bring people together.

To me, all this meant I needed to try to be a solid citizen no matter how I was viewed by others—successful at work, at continued self-improvement, and in my service to others. "Solid Citizen" became an aspiration of mine after hearing Sam articulate this so many times over the years. *(I'm still working on this to this day, by the way!)*

I always thought it was easy to rationalize the first two because it was such a direct connection to our business results and in the end that is what I thought I got hired to do. The third one—to give back to our community—was more for the brand and a nod to the notion that if you are successful in the first two objectives—it's your *responsibility* to give back to the community. If you were successful, and if you did well in your career, it was your responsibility to give back to your community.

But what does it really mean to give back to your community? Stroke a check once a year to a charity from extra money after the bills were paid? Maybe bid on a few items from the United Way rally every year? Or was it giving to your church every Sunday and call it good? What does it really mean to "give back to your community"? What does it mean to be a "solid citizen" while you are striving to lead a good career and a more fulfilling life?

From as early as I can remember to my days through college, I had no clue of what it meant to think much of anything other than myself. In my youth, inexperience, and selfish ways, I led my life as if I were holding a rake in my hand. Whatever I could rake in that helped me was what I did—sports, school, work, hanging out with friends, and just about every waking hour was spent thinking about how the sun rose and set on my view of the world. Writing these words at this stage of my life kind of stings but it's the truth.

I think back to those days now and over time I forgave myself for how unaware I was of my impact on other people's lives due to my youthful arrogance.

Over time that changed, and I began to be aware of my impact on others. Maybe I was maturing, maybe I was just getting tired of my youthful obsessions, maybe my parent's prayers were answered. I remember feeling things changing when I got my first job out of college. Soon after that marriage came upon me, and a few years after that, children. Something about a serious job, marriage, and kids seems to drive a certain amount of maturity in one's life.

I remember when I started volunteering at a social club in Waterloo. My wife and I started donating time to young couples who were preparing to be married. We started giving financial support regularly to our church. I was slowly but surely starting to give back long before Sam Allen gave me that advice.

Later in life, I became involved more and more in community activities. I joined Trout Unlimited as a lifetime member. Joining the board of directors for the Technology Association of Iowa was a great experience. Later, I joined the board for the Wildwood Hills Ranch of Iowa—a great organization founded by people of such strong faith it inspired me. Wildwood Hills Ranch of Iowa is dedicated to serving kids aged 8 to 18 who come from the toughest of all social situations, providing them hope and healing. I started mentoring people in various parts of their career. I started guest lecturing at the University of Iowa, University of Northern

Iowa, and Morningside College. For seven years, I coached my daughter's soccer teams. My wife was equally engaged in serving as a treasurer for a local women's transition home—Beacon of Life, as well as treasurer of both the Dowling Catholic High School Soccer and Volleyball Clubs for many years. Since 1996, every month, without exception, we have sent money to children in the Philippines and every four months, we write them letters or receive letters from them.

As I reflect back on these experiences, there is no denying the positive influence they had on me. I gained as much (or more) from these experiences than the organizations did.

If I defined success by how much I could rake in for my own benefit I'd be stuck in my early, selfish, twenties. I'd still be looking at the world in a "what's in it for me" worldview. But those days are long gone. Success today is about being significant, not to myself, but to those around me. Have I been there for others during times of need? When I could have made a difference in someone's life, did I? If I were gone tomorrow, would anyone notice that I was gone? Do I matter to anyone else I this world? How have I used my gifts and successes to advance others? How have I "given back go my community" as Sam would have stated it?

Strangely writing this book is a step in this journey as well: Trying to share my story, the story of so many others, and the leading practices I've come across over my life so that you can benefit, build upon, and do more in your life. In some small way, maybe something you read in this book will be meaningful to your life. If so, you've helped me become the citizen I was meant to be. Maybe someday you will be able to help others as well.

In the end, with true citizenship in action, you will move forward, always onward and upward, and the world will be better for it.

Leading Practices

What does it truly mean to be a "citizen" in today's day and age? In ancient Greece, it meant that you owned land, were entitled to vote, and were subject to military service if the country so needed you. Later in world history, it's been associated in Western cultures by duty to your fellow citizens. Still a more detailed definition is centered on whether you have the legal right to reside in a given country, as in "are you a citizen or an alien of a given country?"

Merriam Webster's also defines citizenship as "the qualities that a person is expected to have as a responsible member of a community." This is the definition we will use in this book. Going another step further, we want to dial it down to the individual level. Specifically, how does becoming a better citizen relate to leading a successful career and a more fulfilling life?

Becoming a good citizen has meaning in two key areas of our lives. One is a state of being, as in "I am a trustworthy person." All the qualities and values you carry in your life help make you the person you are. This reflects on how others view you and by extension on how others view your citizenship. A second state is one of action. How do you participate in your community? For example, you may engage in politics, support community improvement efforts, or serve on a public or nonprofit board.

For our purposes today, it's important to acknowledge two key aspects of citizenship—one of "being" and a second of "doing."

Citizenship as a State of "Doing"

In 2018, the Pew Center Research Center asked Americans what it means to be a good citizen. (See the figure in the following page). Note the many aspects of life included in the responses from voting in elections, to jury duty, to displaying the American flag. No matter where you are in the world these types of patriotic citizenship activities are a good list of activities to include in your day-to-day life.

A few other aspects of being a good citizen might include:

- *Care for our environment*: Reduce, reuse, or recycle where possible, in that order. Never pollute and support organizations that make life more sustainable.
- *Volunteer your time*: To the extent that you can afford to, be generous with your time and talent in your community. It is often a rewarding experience with the benefits flowing both ways.

**Voting, paying taxes, following law rank
highest as good citizenship traits**

*% who say it is____ important to what it means to be a
good citizen to ...*

	■Very	■Somewhat	NET
Vote in elections	74		91
Pay all the taxes you owe	71		92
Always follow the law	69		96
Serve jury duty if called	61		89
Respect the opinions of those who disagree	61		92
Participate in the U.S. census every decade	60		88
Volunteer to help others	52		90
Know the pledge of allegiance	50		75
Follow what happens in govt. and politics	49		90
protest if you think govt. actions are wrong	45		82
Display the American flag	36		62

Source: Survey of U.S. adults conducted January 29 to February 13, 2018, PEW Research Center.

- *Share your treasure*: As your wealth builds and you take care of essentials like food, clothing, retirement, and other family expenses think about what you can give to others. A good starting point is aiming for 10 percent of your take home pay—or tithing in some cultures.
- *Be active in your community*: Know what's going on in your community and engage in the areas that you find interesting. Support people and organizations who are trying to make your community a better place.
- *Being a good neighbor*: Have good relations whenever possible with those you live with. Take your neighbors' welfare into consideration as if their experiences were your own. Scoop the snow for an elderly neighbor, organize a dinner group, or simply wave and say hello when you see them.
- *Be knowledgeable about the world*: As the world continues to get smaller and smaller with technology and social media, become a consumer of world events. Link these events to how it impacts

your life and those in your community. With the recent COVID pandemic, this has never been more important than it is today.

- *Serving the public*: Lead, or support those in public leadership roles. Our mayors, governors, police, firefighters, and other public servants need community support to be effective in their roles. If the spirit so moves you to a vocation in any of these jobs you will know what we mean by this. If not, it would be wise to support leaders in your community.

Citizenship as a State of "Being"

What are the core values that define you today? My guess is these are also what others appreciate about you as well. When you think about the best version of yourself, what comes to mind?

Below is a table that you can reflect on from JamesClear.com. James recommends that you select up to five to focus on because "if everything is a core value, then nothing is a priority." Taking some time to peruse this list, think about what is important in your life, and identifying five to focus on is a great place to start. Keep this book handy and revisit this chapter and the list below to see how your priorities change over time.

Authenticity	Creativity	Knowledge	Respect
Achievement	Curiosity	Leadership	Responsibility
Adventure	Determination	Learning	Security
Authority	Fairness	Love	Self-respect
Autonomy	Faith	Loyalty	Service
Balance	Fame	Meaningful work	Spirituality
Justice	Friendships	Openness	Stability
Boldness	Fun	Optimism	Success
Compassion	Growth	Peace	Status
Challenge	Happiness	Pleasure	Trustworthiness
Citizenship	Honesty	Poise	Wealth
Community	Humor	Popularity	Wisdom
Competency	Influence	Recognition	Reputation
Contribution	Inner harmony	Religion	Kindness

Source: JamesClear.com

Common Themes of "Being" and "Doing"

- *The Common Good*: Ever since Aristotle coined the phrase "the common interest" around ~ 350 BC, human beings have been developing ways to deal with issues that benefit everyone in society. Any individual in society contributes in some way to the common good of the community. Sometimes this is through the payment of taxes for roads, bridges, maintenance, and other community services. As an individual, it's important to know that you both contribute to and receive benefits from "the common good."

- *Sacrifice*: Sometimes doing what is convenient isn't always the best route to take in the long run. At times, you will need to sacrifice your short-term and/or personal priorities for the benefit of the long-term and/or greater good. Thinking about how you feel about where this balance lies is a good idea.

- *Change*: Most likely your priorities will change over time. As your career evolves and your role in the world takes shape, it's good to acknowledge that you don't need to have it all figured out at all times. But this could change once you get a promotion, get married, or have kids. You can also have setbacks, get laid off, lose a loved one, or have some other surprise come at you that you didn't expect. Whether they are good or bad, events in life will most certainly guarantee that things will change, and with them so must you.

Service

It's becoming a cliche these days to talk about servant leadership styles, but there really is some magic to the concept behind that. In a servant-led organization, the CEO works for the senior staff, the senior staff works for their team, and on down the organization. Ultimately, the job of servant leadership is to support the needs of the people who report to them, remove impediments, and help the organization succeed by living a life of service to the organization.

A mentor of Tony's, Barry Schaffter, once told him in 2000, "You really only have 1 job in the company, and that's to serve the customers. If you are so privileged to have a job leading people, you might have two jobs—serve customers and your team".

Shared Wisdom: Lessons From the Road

The *Desiderata* is a poem that was originally published in the early 1920s that might help you think about your broader place in society (among many other thoughts) and recommends many ways to both "be" and "do" good in our society.

Go placidly amid the noise and the haste, and remember what peace there may be in silence. As far as possible, without surrender, be on good terms with all persons. Speak your truth quietly and clearly; and listen to others, even to the dull and the ignorant; they too have their story. Avoid loud and aggressive persons; they are vexatious to the spirit. If you compare yourself with others, you may become vain or bitter, for always there will be greater and lesser persons than yourself. Enjoy your achievements as well as your plans. Keep interested in your own career, however humble; it is a real possession in the changing fortunes of time. Exercise caution in your business affairs, for the world is full of trickery. But let this not blind you to what virtue there is; many persons strive for high ideals, and everywhere life is full of heroism. Be yourself. Especially do not feign affection. Neither be cynical about love; for in the face of all aridity and disenchantment it is as perennial as the grass. Take kindly the counsel of the years, gracefully surrendering the things of youth. Nurture strength of spirit to shield you in sudden misfortune. But do not distress yourself with dark imaginings. Many fears are born of fatigue and loneliness. Beyond a wholesome discipline, be gentle with yourself. You are a child of the universe no less than the trees and the stars; you have a right to be here. And whether or not it is clear to you, no doubt the universe is unfolding as it should. Therefore be at peace with God, whatever you conceive Him to be. And whatever your labors and aspirations, in the noisy confusion of life, keep peace in your soul. With all its sham, drudgery, and broken dreams, it is still a beautiful world. Be cheerful. Strive to be happy.

—Max Ehrmann, American writer
Desiderata, 1927

Stan, an executive in the agriculture industry, shares advice he received about getting involved in a community and treating it like you would live there forever.

A former employee told me to remember that as I move with the company, I'd be bringing along my wife and kids. The kids would adapt easily with new friends, but we needed to get my wife involved in the new community as quickly as possible. Best advice ever! We knew at each move that the goal was to live in the new place like it was forever. Kept my wife sane and life at home much smoother while I traveled around.

—Stan Vardell, VP Parts Operations
Greenway Equipment, Arkansas, USA

Kirk shares how his career evolved from city administration to private and then back to public service as mayor and how important it is to build relationships deep in the community.

My leadership career began at the age of 23 when I became City Administrator of my home town. I was in the public eye daily and had to mature quickly. I resolved that challenge by listening, seeking out mentors and "always showing up." I was prepared, positive, people-oriented and built relationships even in times of disagreement. Seven years later I was recruited to run the local bank in town and later voted in as Mayor, which validated the trust I had developed with the community.

—Kirk Bjorland, Realtor
Coldwell Bankers: Iowa, USA

Kelly, a mental health counselor, shares the importance of volunteering and serving on local nonprofit organizations.

I also feel that volunteering and serving on nonprofit and church boards has absolutely provided a deep understanding of flexing, adjusting, learning, and growing. In addition, attending and participating in networking or learning events outside the company are extremely rewarding. Being with others going through similar situations allows me to feel confident in all I know (sometimes we don't get that at work) and also provides a safe environment to ask questions and seek guidance and best practices.

—Kelly Kreiter Penning
Mental Health Counselor at Family Resources and Executive
Director of New Kingdom Trailriders
Iowa, USA

Michelle, who left a very successful career in public policy for a major Fortune 50 company to lead a nonprofit, shares how important being active in volunteering has been to her career.

I would have become a community volunteer sooner. As it was, I waited until my kids were out of school to become active. The people I've met through volunteerism have made a huge difference in my career. Giving back has given me satisfaction that day-to-day work didn't. And I would have set a better example for my children.

—Michelle Book, President and CEO
Food Bank of Iowa, Iowa, USA

Jeff, a mechanical engineer out of college who followed his passion for Six Sigma to pioneer efficiency improvements in health care, shares how important he believes it is to be the leader your community needs.

Do not be afraid to change your course or make a move into something new. Embrace new programs, technology, and initiatives. Be the leader your organization or community needs to champion positive change and good things will happen. Pioneering is more fulfilling than simply following others.

—Jeff Rich, Executive Director
Gundersen Lutheran Health Systems, Wisconsin, USA

Don't worry about the level of individual prominence you have achieved; worry about the individuals you have helped become better people. This is my final recommendation: Think about the metric by which your life will be judged, and make a resolution to live every day so that in the end, your life will be judged a success.

—Clayton Christensen (1952–2020)
Harvard Business Review "How will you measure your life" 2010

Reflections: What's Your Story?

1. What are your main insights/takeaways from the chapter at this moment?

_____

_____

_____

_____

_____

_____

_____

_____

_____

2. What are one to three goals/intentions you would like to set for yourself?

_____

_____

_____

_____

_____

_____

_____

_____

_____

_____

Going Further: Questions, Readings, and References

Discussion Questions

17.1   Tony talked about his realization that it's a responsibility to give back to our communities. What can you get involved in the next 30 days to take a step in that direction?

17.2   What parts of "The Desiderata" speak to you the most? Make a note to revisit this poem in a year and jot down any changes.

17.3   Part of being a good citizen is an act of "being" that reflect more on your core values. What would you say are your core values? What would someone who knows you well say your core values are?

17.4   In what ways can you improve the "common good" in your workplace, neighborhood, or city?

17.5   What does living in a sustainable world mean to you? How can you participate in making the world a better, more sustainable, place to live?

Suggested Reading

Aronson, B. 2020. *Human Kind: Changing the World One Small Act at a Time.* Canada: LifeTree Media.

Brookings Institute. 2019. www.brookings.edu/blog/education-plus-development/ 2019/11/12/the-bucket-list-for-involved-citizens-76-things-you-can-do-to-boost-civic-engagement

MacAskill, W. 2016. *Doing Good Better: How Effective Altruism Can Help You Help Others, Do Work that Matters, and Make Smarter Choices about Giving Back.* New York, NY: Avery.

Maxwell, J., and R. Hoskins. 2021. *Change Your World: How Anyone, Anywhere Can Make a Difference.* Nashville: HarperCollins Leadership.

References

Merriam-Webster. 2022. "Citizenship." www.merriam-webster.com

Pew Research Center. 2018. *The Public, the Political System and American Democracy.* Washington, D.C.

www.jamesclear.com

CHAPTER 18

Finances

FINANCES
BUDGET
INVEST
LEARN
TEAMWORK

Compound Interest is the eighth wonder of the world. He who understands it, earns it. He who doesn't, pays it.

—Albert Einstein
Theoretical physicist

Introduction

Having a solid understanding of the basics of personal finances will play at least two important roles in your life. First, it will help you optimize the financial reward from the hard work and accomplishments of your career as your income grows. How you handle success, and your growth in income, will loom large over your lifetime. Second, it will play an enabling role to open you up to more experiences if you manage financial resources appropriately. If you spend money on more experiences, and experiences lead to more learning and growth, then money will help you learn and grow faster than others.

Knowing that you need to be financially savvy early in your career will pay you dividends in huge ways down the road. Not only will you have time on your side for your investments to grow, but you will develop the right habits early so when your income grows you have the discipline needed to build true long-term wealth. It's wise to make financial acumen a core part of your foundation for many, many reasons.

Tony's Lessons From Personal Experience

I remember helping my grandfather pick up branches and rocks in a grove of trees when I was six or seven years old. He paid me a quarter and I thought I was rich. I remember when I was nine or ten going around the neighborhood selling personalized Christmas cards door to door. I deeply wanted a fishing rod and tacklebox they had as one of the awards. When I was 12, a bike ride came through town called RAGBRAI (Register's Annual Great Bike Ride Across Iowa) and a friend and I set up a lemonade stand under some shade trees and sold ham sandwiches. The $40 I made that day was my first deposit in my first ever bank account. On many occasions, when school was called due to a snowstorm I went along with my father on his sales route delivering beer all over western Iowa. When I was in high school from age 15, I worked at a Fareway Grocery store most mornings from 6 to 8 a.m. until I graduated high school. During the summers I detasseled and walked beans most days, mowed lawns during the day, or worked the night shift picking orders for a convenience store delivery company. I had lots of opportunities to learn the value of hard work and managing money as a kid.

Making money and saving it was kind of a way of life for me from a very young age. So it was only natural that when I started working for John Deere at the age of 20 that I continued it. One of the first influences in my professional life was a supervisor on the shop floor named Max Schreiber. Max was a Marine (one of the things he taught me is there's no such thing as an "ex-Marine") who ran a department that bonded brake pads on steel brake plates. I was assigned as a process engineer to improve the processes they used.

One day Max took me aside and gave me a great piece of advice. He said,

Sign up and start contributing to your 401(k). The company will match some of it, and your earnings will grow for the rest of your life. You are not going to miss it at your age, and it'll be the easiest money you ever make in your life.

I have to say, 34 years later, Max was right. Most years the company matched my 401(k) up to a certain percent and I'm grateful I heeded Max's advice.

In 2001 my wife and I were at odds financially. We were making good money for our ages, starting to raise a family, drove relatively new cars, and lived in a nice home. We had started to accumulate sizable savings and were investing more through payroll deduction. However, we had a fundamentally different way of viewing taxes that led to fairly regular disagreements throughout the year but especially during tax time. In a nutshell, she held a very conservative view of tax regulations where if there was a gray area, we ended up paying more in taxes. I seemed to always want to find the legal ways to minimize our taxes.

It was around that time when we hired a financial advisor. The real story is we hired an "arbiter" who would be the tiebreaker when we had disagreements on how much we owed in taxes. We had three main criteria for a financial advisor: first, that they be "fee only" as we weren't interested in hearing sales pitches for investments that they received a kickback on. Second, they had to be a certified financial planner through a reputable agency. Lastly, and most importantly from my perspective, they had to be an expert in U.S. tax policy.

One of the biggest concerns I had was that we had overpaid our taxes, so the first job we gave our financial planner was to review our last three years of tax returns and if he could find his first year's fees, we would agree to take him on as our financial advisor. After providing our returns, he came back to us three weeks later with amended tax forms that not only covered his first year's fees but also covered his first four years' fees! Both my wife and I were elated as the money was a huge unexpected benefit. We didn't care who was right or wrong and it helped bring us closer together as a team when it came to our finances.

From that point on, it became the three of us debating various positions and working together to find the right path forward for all our financial decisions. That's been our formula from day one and it is what we use today as we sort through living wills, trusts, estate planning, investments, insurance, charitable giving, and a myriad of other financial issues.

No one will ever care about your finances as much as you do, so you might as well become knowledgeable and take ownership early in your career. As your earnings grow, things tend to get more complex, especially when it comes to managing your money. Your financial literacy should also continue to grow as well, up to and including asking for help along the way.

Money isn't generally the answer to your problems, but it can create a few if you don't manage it right. It's best to start out right and put time on your side, learn as much as you can, seek help from experts, and work at it as a team.

Leading Practices

A big reason why financial literacy became a part of this book is because of the feedback we received from so many people in the early drafts we provided to senior-level college students and those early in their professional careers. We quickly understood it was a major gap that we had to close if our book was to be helpful to today's modern professionals. It just meant too much professionally and personally not to address it.

Tony's stories point to salient lessons we can all use to help us in our financial literacy. Let's review five important concepts and how you can apply them in your life.

- Living at (or below) your means
- Paying yourself first
- Become financially knowledgeable
- Teaming up on finances and ask for help
- Money will not buy you happiness

Living at or Below Your Means

Tony didn't buy fancy cars or things he couldn't afford. Knowing the difference between a "want" and a "need" is helpful here. Early in your career, it's tempting to show the world your early success, take out loans, buy more of a house than what you need, or travel to exotic places. It's even more tempting to justify all of this as normal in today's modern era. Dave Ramsey perhaps says it best when he promotes only spending the money you have and not going into debt: "If you live like no one else, later on in life you will truly live like no one else." What he means here is don't fall for the trap of going into debt—live below your means, and someday you will have so much money that you will be able to live like no one else.

Paying Yourself First

The first 10 percent of Tony's pretax salary went to his 401(k) for his retirement, the next 10 percent went to charity, the next 10 percent went to savings, and then he paid bills. He started this process during his intern years when he was just 20 years old. Just like Tony's first boss Max Schreiber told him to set savings aside and forget about it, the best practice is to use payroll deduction to make savings a process and not a decision each pay period. Make one decision—to invest early in your future, then use a system like payroll deduction to execute that one decision, and your financial fortunes will improve.

Become Financially Knowledgeable

Tony went to Charles Given's seminars in the 1990s to learn about no load mutual funds. He read books like *Rich Dad, Poor Dad*. He invested in passive income businesses and started his own businesses a few times. He and his wife continue to read books, invest in learning about new financial tools, and continue to work as a team. All of this helped build their financial proficiency and led to better decisions being made throughout his career.

One note of caution: *what you don't know can hurt you*. Be curious, learn from others, and when you don't understand something ask questions. Missing a tax deduction can cost you hundreds and maybe thousands of dollars. Not knowing about a matching funds opportunity for your company's 401(k) program can hurt you. Buying a car or home by only looking at the monthly payment or mortgage amount and not understanding the interest being charged can hurt you. Not knowing about a change in tax law can do the same. Not having a will can cost you and your loved ones in the long run. It always pays to learn more about financial literacy and take the time to be curious and ask a few more questions when it comes to your finances.

Team Up on Your Finances and Ask for Help

Tony hired a "fee only" financial planner when he was 33 to help develop and build a strong financial plan. He and his wife Sheila have maintained that plan for over 20 years. While the initial hiring of the advisor was to help them make decisions around payment of taxes, the wealth of advice he provided over the years helped accelerate Tony's financial literacy. It was some of the best money he ever spent and was well worth it in the long run.

Tony's wife was an accountant, and he was an engineer. Together, they pooled their finances and teamed up to manage them. Each of them brought a unique view to financial literacy, and while they never agreed on everything, they were committed to each other and worked together as a team.

Money Will Not Buy You Happiness

It's quite the cliché and we truly believe it—money cannot buy you happiness. However, the absence of money may lead to unhappiness and unnecessary anxiety, pain, and suffering throughout your lifetime. A lot of marriages end from financial conflicts. Honest and good people sometimes make bad decisions when they are financially stressed. The world can be a dark, dangerous, and very sad place when it comes to poor financial management or lack of financial literacy. Without proper planning and financial acumen, you may be forced to make decisions you would not have otherwise had to make. A lot of these types of situations stem from trying to live beyond your means, taking too much risk with debt, and trying to live someone else's lifestyle as your own trying to impress others.

Happiness is a much larger pursuit in life than having the biggest bank account in the world. We've touched on the importance of balance earlier in the book and we'd suggest everyone has an opportunity to balance their financial aspirations against living a happy and fulfilling life. Setting good financial goals should also be a habit early in your career. Some good goals to consider can be how much you save as a percent of your pay, eliminating debt in the long run, investing for retirement, being generous to charity, and allocating a certain amount of savings to enjoy the journey.

There are many other aspects of financial literacy that can be gleaned from many smart people. Take advantage of all you can and set a goal to be a lifelong learner when it comes to financial literacy.

Shared Wisdom: Lessons From the Road

Entire books and industries are dedicated to financial literacy and as you would expect our experts had plenty of great advice for what to do when starting out in your career.

Noel, an innovator and intellectual property lead for a major Fortune 100 company, shares his four-point recipe for success.

> *Live well within your means so you can (1) share something with those in need, (2) avoid credit card and other debt on depreciating assets, (3) save a lot for retirement, (4) maintain an emergency fund.*
> —Noel Anderson, Intellectual Property Lead
> John Deere, North Dakota, USA

Gary, a retired chief information officer of a Fortune 100 company, shares the power of establishing a long-term view of your career and your view to your personal finances, and how this can shape intentional investments in your growth as well as develop good financial habits.

> *Track your net worth and the amount that you give back (through volunteerism and donations) every year, starting from the beginning of your career. I like the idea of tracking net worth as a way to incent saving, investing wisely and avoiding unnecessary debt—and you can see progress over time. It also helps in making conscious choices to invest in your future (e.g., education, changing jobs, etc.) in that you may see net worth appropriately go down for a few years while making*

that investment. I like tracking giving back to keep a focus on giving back and to watch progress over time.

—Gary Scholten, Chief Information Technology Officer
(Retired)
Principal Financial Group, Iowa, USA

Richard, president of a personal financial services firm, shares the power of living for today and planning for tomorrow.

One of the main keys to lifetime financial success is finding the balance between living for today and planning for tomorrow. If you spend everything you make plus 10 percent more, you will have no financial future. If you save everything but the bare necessities, you miss out on enjoying today.

—Richard Salmen, President
Family Investment Center, Missouri, USA

Brian, a senior software engineer, shares his powerful observation of the connection between engaging in manual labor to improve your life and how this can contribute to saving money by lowering your cost of living.

Learn how to change your vehicle's oil, air filter, and replace a battery. Learn how to maintain your own lawn equipment. Learn how to fix a toilet, a leaky pipe, a clogged shower head. Take your computer apart and put it back together again. The things you own will own you unless you take the time to understand how they work. Intentionally decide what tasks/jobs are worth delegating to others and which give you joy and worthwhile skills. Get your hands dirty. It's ok. There is plenty of soap available. Fix and maintain your own stuff... and then use those skills to help as well as teach others in need. The higher your curiosity, the lower your cost of living. Who knows, you might just awaken something in your mind that unlocks paths you never anticipated.

—Brian Smith, Senior Software Writer
John Deere, Illinois, USA

Scott, a senior vice president of a marketing firm, shares great advice on managing personal finances that have a substantial influence in your long-term wealth.

Never carry a credit card balance forward if at all possible. If unable to pay it all, save every penny, eating mac and cheese or whatever it takes—to get it paid off.

Max out that 401k from day one if you have the option. If not, have 15 percent of your income automatically drafted and invested into a Vanguard (low fee) Total Stock Market mutual fund forever and ever. Make it untouchable.

Avoid all debt except the home mortgage.

Keep driving that old car. Pride makes you want a new one but redirect that pride so that the car represents maturity, practicality, and wisdom.

I think these are important because none of us can really understand compounding well. But all we really need to know is the importance of time. It's best to put even that small amount of money to work early so that it has time to work its magic.

—Scott Burleson, Senior Vice President
AIM Institute, North Carolina, USA

Guarav, a director of an IT firm in India, shares his observation on the power of paying yourself (and hence investing) first.

I would share a magic formula of expenses = earning—savings. It means save first then spend the remaining. Not vice versa!

—Guarav Gupta, Director
Yash Technologies, Pune, India

Reflections: What's Your Story?

1. What are your main insights/takeaways from the chapter at this moment?

_____

_____

_____

_____

_____

_____

_____

_____

_____

2. What are one to three goals/intentions you would like to set for yourself?

_____

_____

_____

_____

_____

_____

_____

_____

_____

Going Further: Questions, Readings, and References

Discussion Questions

18.1 What are your own personal values when it comes to managing money and how have they influenced your decisions about personal finances?

18.2 What is your personal financial net worth? What changes could you make tomorrow to make a positive impact on it over time?

18.3 Looking back on your last 30 days' expenses what do you notice about your spending habits? Do you pay yourself first (save and invest) and do you use your money on purchases wisely?

18.4 When is the last time that you were truly generous with your finances? How did that make you feel versus the feeling of earning money?

18.5 Take 15 minutes and write down five financial goals for the next 12 months, the next five years, and lifetime goals. Store this list where you can access them over time and update them. What did you achieve? What doesn't matter anymore? What needs to be added? Who can help you achieve your goals?

Suggested Reading

Danford, D. 2020. *Happy to Be Different—Personal and Money Success Through Better Thinking*. Sarasota, FL: First Edition Design and Publishing.

Housel, M. 2020. *The Psychology of Money*. Petersfield, Hampshire: Harriman House Publishing.

Kiyosaki, R.T. 2017. *Rich Dad, Poor Dad*. 20th Anniversary ed. Scottsdale, AZ: Plata Publishing.

Lynch, P. 1996. *Learn to Earn: A Beginner's Guide to Investing and Business*. New York, NY: Simon and Schuster.

Sethi, R. 2019. *I Will Teach You to be Rich*. 2nd ed. New York, NY: Workman Publishing.

Siegel, C. 2018. *Why Didn't They Teach Me This in School? 99 Personal Money Principles to Live By*. North Charleston, SC: CreateSpace Independent Publishing Platform.

Conclusions and Celebrations

In our introduction we indicated that you are indeed a "coauthor" of this book by how you react to the material presented and integrate it into your life. We believe this book is not complete without your notes in the margins and your use of the concepts in your own situation.

In Chapter 13 on Adversity, we introduced the concept of E+R=O, or Event + Reaction = Outcome. In its simplest form, the event was your reading this book, and the outcome or result cannot be determined until you determine how you will react to it. Then, and only then, can you truly know how this book made a difference in your life.

By now, we hope you understand our intentions and that you have actively played the part of a coauthor. We hope the experience has started to make a difference in your life and has led you to explore your personal and professional development in a new light.

Take a moment to stop and reflect and celebrate the new beginning of the rest of your life! Take what you have learned, add it to your experiences, and go forward with a newfound confidence and zeal for becoming the best you can possibly be! Take the time to enjoy the journey along the way. *Don't focus so much on the future that you forget the joy of today.*

Please continue to revisit these lessons to reactivate additional learning and write more notes in the margins to personalize and memorialize your journey.

You should also by now have a good understanding of the value of asking "Am I Doing This Right?" not as an indication of weakness but as a seed of strength leading to deeper understanding of how to grow a successful career and lead a more fulfilling life.

Is This All There Is to It?

There are many debatable aspects of career development and certainly we could have included more topics. However, in our research, our collective experience, and in the feedback received, we believe the topics we addressed represent a solid list of issues that are critical at the beginning of any career.

As your career grows and life becomes more complex, different issues will emerge that present the promise of exciting growth as well as the perils of more headaches. Within these joys and struggles lie professional challenges such as more responsibilities in your job, leading other people in their career, changing jobs, more senior-level executive experiences, dealing with setbacks in positive and constructive ways, and many, many other topics.

At the same time, you will most likely find changes to your personal life in your relationships, the potential for marriage and children, a higher level of interaction in your community, and a more advanced understanding of who you are and what your impact on the world is.

Even greater pressures emerge when you think about mid-career or senior-level stages of your career. Strategic thinking, leading large organizations, dealing with constant change, recruiting and developing high-potential talent, determining succession plans for critical roles, the art of delegating, and making complex decisions and so many more issues present challenges in the latter stages of a career. At the same time, at a personal level, your thoughts shift from being successful to what your legacy will be and how your contributions will make a difference for others after you retire.

These mid-career and senior-level issues present challenges of their own. The concepts presented in this book are meant to serve as a base foundation for a strong career and a more fulfilling life by focusing on early career development. We have plans to address issues that are critical to mid-career and senior-level professional development in future editions of *Am I Doing This Right?*

We also designed each chapter around a key topic, providing well-balanced, concise, relevant insights, tools, and advice regarding each topic. Each chapter should provide you a space to focus on the topic at hand and lead you to a deeper understanding of how the topic impacts your life and career. But in the end, it's how this book impacts your whole person that counts.

The *"Whole Person Concept"* is the reality that no single idea, decision, or characteristic will automatically define you completely. You are way more than any individual element—furthermore, you are way more than the sum of individual pieces. You are the "complete person," and all of your experiences, day-in and day-out, continue to propel your development.

We hope this book has helped you become a "more complete person" indeed!

Closing Thoughts and Next Steps

It's our sincere hope that your career and life have changed as a result of reading this book. To continue to gain the most from this book, we recommend taking the following actions:

- *Stay active and keep this book handy…* to revisit often as your career and experiences grow. As you make decisions in your life, and as the world continues to change, the lessons in this book will take on new meanings.
- *Pass along what you learned…* by sharing the insights from this book with others. The power of your reaction to this book is significant to you and to those with whom you share it. You will learn more as you talk about your reactions to this book.
- *Invest in someone's career…* by sending a copy of this book to someone you care about. They may be a college or high school graduate, someone taking on a new role, or people struggling to get their feet underneath them in the beginning of their professional journey. If your company has an onboarding program, this book would make an ideal addition to the process. If you teach a class to college students, this would make an excellent addition to their reading list.
- Order individual copies on Amazon or contact Business Expert Press for bulk business or academic orders.

- Connect with us! Follow Tony, Matthew, and Jeffrey on social media and let's help each other get better every day.
- Visit www.doingthisrightbooks.com to share your story so others can gain from your personal experience.
- Sign up for monthly newsletters that connect community members to the latest trends in personal development, stories that share experiences, and insights from the authors.
- Write to us and let us know how this book helped you or someone close to you. We are working hard on future editions for mid- and senior-level careers and value your feedback.

Lastly, we sincerely hope this really isn't the conclusion or the "end" of the book as far as how it has influenced your career and life. *We hope it's the beginning of something great.*

Sincerely,
Tony Thelen
Matthew Mitchell
Jeffrey Kappen
October 2022

About the Authors

Tony D. Thelen is the Chief Product Officer for John Deere Financial. His 34-year career includes a wide variety of leadership roles spanning manufacturing, sales, marketing, operations, technology, strategy, and finance. Tony is a certified executive coach from the Neuro Leadership Institute, a member of the International Federation of Coaching, and an affiliate of the Institute of Coaching and Co-Active Training Institute. Tony holds a bachelor's degree in chemical engineering from Iowa State University, an MBA from the University of Northern Iowa, and a postgraduate diploma in strategy and innovation from Oxford University. Tony is a National Council member of the Roaring Fork Conservancy and a lifetime member of Trout Unlimited. Tony and his wife, Sheila, have three daughters. He currently fishes and writes from his home on West Okoboji Lake in northwest Iowa.

Matthew C. Mitchell is an Associate Professor of International Business and Strategy at Drake University, and a founding partner of Bâton Global, a consulting firm providing strategy, innovation, leadership, and research services that transform organizations worldwide. Matthew has travelled, lived and worked in more than 75 countries and has advised companies, governments, and nonprofits throughout the world. He is a regular commentator on issues such as innovation, globalization, and firm strategy. Matthew earned degrees in physics, math and an MBA from Rollins College. He earned his PhD in International Business from the University of South Carolina—the world's leading program in international business. Matthew and his wife, Betsy, have three children and currently live in Des Moines, Iowa.

Jeffrey A. Kappen is a founding partner of Bâton Global, a research-driven advisory firm working in the areas of strategy, leadership, and innovation. This includes serving as an advisor and consultant to private and public sector organizations supporting them with the development and execution of their global strategies, leadership development programs, and market analysis. Concurrent to his leadership role at Bâton Global, Jeffrey is also Associate Professor of Management and International Business at Drake University. In addition to teaching in the areas of leadership, management, global studies, and sustainable development, he maintains an active research agenda on the formation of transnational partnerships, the influence of culture and religion on business, and diversity in organizations. Jeffrey is active in the community serving on the boards of organizations focused on financial literacy, international relations, and youth empowerment. Jeffrey holds a BA with honors in International Relations, French, and Russian from Beloit College, an MBA from the University of Wisconsin, and a PhD in Management and Organization Studies from the University of Massachusetts.

Index

OTHER TITLES IN THE BUSINESS CAREER DEVELOPMENT COLLECTION

Vilma Barr, Consultant, Editor

- *Telling Your Story, Building Your Brand* by Henry Wong
- *Remaining Relevant* by Karen Lawson
- *Pay Attention!* by Cassandra Bailey and Dana M. Schmidt
- *Social Media is About People* by Cassandra Bailey
- *Burn Ladders. Build Bridges.* by Alan M. Patterson
- *Decoding Your STEM Career* by Peter Devenyi
- *A Networking Playbook* by Darryl Howes
- *The Street-Smart Side of Business* by Tara Acosta
- *Rules Don't Work for Me* by Gail Summers
- *Fast Forward Your Career* by Simonetta Lureti and Lucio Furlani
- *Shaping Your Future* by Rita Rocker
- *Emotional Intelligence at Work* by Richard M. Contino and Penelope J. Holt
- *How to Use Marketing Techniques to Get a Great Job* by Edward Barr
- *Negotiate Your Way to Success* by Kasia Jagodzinska
- *How to Make Good Business Decisions* by J.C. Baker
- *Ask the Right Questions; Get the Right Job* by Edward Barr
- *Personal and Career Development* by Claudio A. Rivera and Elza Priede
- *Your GPS to Employment Success* by Beverly A. Williams

Concise and Applied Business Books

The Collection listed above is one of 30 business subject collections that Business Expert Press has grown to make BEP a premiere publisher of print and digital books. Our concise and applied books are for...

- Professionals and Practitioners
- Faculty who adopt our books for courses
- Librarians who know that BEP's Digital Libraries are a unique way to offer students ebooks to download, not restricted with any digital rights management
- Executive Training Course Leaders
- Business Seminar Organizers

Business Expert Press books are for anyone who needs to dig deeper on business ideas, goals, and solutions to everyday problems. Whether one print book, one ebook, or buying a digital library of 110 ebooks, we remain the affordable and smart way to be business smart. For more information, please visit www.businessexpertpress.com, or contact sales@businessexpertpress.com.

CPSIA information can be obtained
at www.ICGtesting.com
Printed in the USA
BVHW030827301022
650608BV00006B/9

9 781637 423172